How to File for Divorce in Texas

with forms

Second Edition

Karen Ann Rolcik
Edward A. Haman
Attorneys at Law

SPHINX® PUBLISHING
A Division of Sourcebooks, Inc.®
Naperville, IL

Second edition, 1998
Information Reviewed, 3/2001

Published by: **Sphinx® Publishing, A Division of Sourcebooks, Inc.®**

<u>Naperville Office</u>
P.O. Box 4410
Naperville, Illinois 60567-4410
630-961-3900
Fax: 630-961-2168

This publication is designed to provide accurate and authoritative information in regard to the subject matter covered. It is sold with the understanding that the publisher is not engaged in rendering legal, accounting, or other professional service. If legal advice or other expert assistance is required, the services of a competent professional person should be sought.

From a Declaration of Principles Jointly Adopted by a Committee of the
American Bar Association and a Committee of Publishers and Associations

This product is not a substitute for legal advice.

Disclaimer required by Texas statutes.

Library of Congress Cataloging-in-Publication Data
Rolcik, Karen Ann.
    How to file for divorce in Texas : with forms / Karen Ann Rolcik,
Edward A. Haman.—2nd ed.
      p.   cm.
    Includes index.
    ISBN 1-57071-330-8 (pbk.)
    1. Divorce suits—Texas—Popular works. 2. Divorce—Law and
legislation—Texas—Popular works. I. Haman, Edward A.￼   II. Title.
KFT1300.Z9R65   1998
346.76401'66—dc21   97-42874
                                                               CIP

Printed and bound in the United States of America.
VHG Paperback — 10 9 8 7 6

CONTENTS

Using Self-Help Law Books

Whenever you shop for a product or service, you are faced with various levels of quality and price. In deciding upon which product or service to buy, you make a cost/value analysis based upon what you are willing to pay and the quality you desire.

When buying a car you decide whether you want transportation, comfort, status, or sex appeal. Accordingly, you decide among such choices as a Neon, a Lincoln, a Rolls Royce, or a Porsche. Before making a decision, you usually weigh the merits of each option against the cost.

When you get a headache, you can take a pain reliever (such as aspirin) or visit a medical specialist for a neurological examination. Given this choice, most people, of course, take a pain reliever, since it costs only pennies, whereas a medical examination costs hundreds of dollars and takes a lot of time. This is usually a logical choice because rarely is anything more than a pain reliever needed for a headache. But in some cases, a headache may indicate a brain tumor, and failing to see a specialist right away can result in complications. Should everyone with a headache go to a specialist? Of course not, but people treating their own illnesses must realize that they are betting, on the basis of their cost/value analysis of the situation, that they are taking the most logical option.

The same cost/value analysis must be made in deciding to do one's own legal work. Many legal situations are very straightforward, requiring a simple form and no complicated analysis. Anyone with a little intelligence and a book of instructions can handle the matter simply.

But there is always the chance that complications are involved that only an attorney would notice. To simplify the law into a book like this, several legal cases often must be condensed into a single sentence or paragraph. Otherwise, the book would be several hundred pages long and too complicated for most people. However, this simplification necessarily leaves out many details and nuances which would apply to special or unusual situations. Also, there are many ways to interpret most legal questions. Your case may come before a judge who disagrees with the analysis of our authors.

Therefore, in deciding to use a self-help law book and to do your own legal work, you must realize that you are making a cost/value analysis, and are deciding that the chance your case will not turn out to your satisfaction is outweighed by the money you will save by doing it yourself. Most people handling their own simple legal matters never have a problem, but occasionally people find that it ended up costing them more to have an attorney straighten out the situation than it would have if they had hired an attorney in the beginning. Keep this in mind while handling your case, and be sure to consult an attorney if you feel you might need further guidance.

INTRODUCTION

Going through a divorce is probably one of the most common, and most traumatic, encounters with the legal system. Paying a divorce lawyer can be one of the most expensive single bills to pay, and at a time when you are least likely to have extra funds. In a contested divorce case it is not uncommon for the parties to run up legal bills of over $10,000; and horror stories abound of lawyers charging substantial fees with little progress to show for it. This book is designed to enable you to obtain a divorce without hiring a lawyer. Even if you do hire a lawyer, this book will help you to work with him or her more effectively, which can also reduce the legal fee.

This is not a law school course, but a practical guide to get you through "the system" as easily as possible. Legal jargon has nearly been eliminated. For ease of understanding, this book uses the term *spouse* to refer to your husband or wife (whichever applies), and the terms *child* and *children* are used interchangeably.

Please keep in mind that different judges, and courts in different counties, may have their own particular (if not peculiar) procedures and ways of doing things. The court clerk's office can often tell you if they have any special forms or requirements. Court clerks cannot give legal advice, but they can tell you what their court or judges require.

The first two chapters of this book will give you an overview of the law and the legal system. Chapters 3, 4, and 5 will help you decide if you want an attorney and if you want a divorce. The remaining chapters will show you what forms you need, how to fill out the forms, and what procedures to follow. You will also find two appendices in the back of the book. Appendix A contains selected portions of the Texas law dealing with various aspects of divorce. Although these provisions are discussed in the book, it is sometimes helpful to read the law exactly as the legislature wrote it.

Finally, appendix B contains the forms you will complete. You will not need to use all of the forms. This book will tell you which forms you need, depending upon your situation. Some forms may need to be changed to fit your particular circumstance.

Be sure to read AN INTRODUCTION TO LEGAL FORMS in chapter 6 before you use any of the forms in this book!

Marriage "Ins and Outs" 1

Several years (or maybe only months) ago you made a decision to get married. This chapter will discuss, in a very general way, what you got yourself into, and how you can get yourself out.

Marriage

Marriage is frequently referred to as a contract. It is a legal contract, and for many, it is also a religious contract. This book will deal only with the legal aspects. The wedding ceremony involves the bride and groom reciting certain vows, that are actually mutual promises about how they will treat each other. There are also legal papers signed, such as a marriage license and a marriage certificate. These formalities create certain rights and obligations for the husband and wife. Although the focus at the ceremony is on the emotional and romantic aspects of the relationship, the legal reality is that financial and property rights are being created. It is these financial and property rights and obligations that cannot be broken without a legal proceeding.

Marriage will give each of the parties certain rights in property, and it creates certain obligations with respect to the support of any children they have together (or adopt). Unfortunately, most people don't fully realize that these rights and obligations are being created until it comes time for a divorce.

DIVORCE

A divorce is the most common method of terminating or breaking the marriage contract. In Texas, a divorce may also be referred to as a *dissolution of marriage*, although the technical legal term is *divorce*. In a divorce, the court declares the marriage contract broken, divides the parties' property and debts, and determines the custody, support, and visitation with respect to any children the parties may have. Traditionally, a divorce could only be granted under certain very specific circumstances, such as for *adultery*, or *mental cruelty*. Today, a divorce may be granted simply because one or both of the parties want one. The wording used to describe the situation is that "the marriage has become insupportable because of discord or conflict of personalities that destroys the legitimate ends of the marriage relationship and prevents any reasonable expectation of reconciliation."

ANNULMENT

The basic difference between a divorce and an annulment is that a divorce says, "this marriage is broken," and an annulment says, "there never was a marriage." An annulment is more difficult and often more complicated to prove, so it is not used very often. Annulments are only possible in a few circumstances, usually where one party deceived the other. If you decide that you want an annulment, you should consult an attorney. If you are seeking an annulment for religious reasons and need to go through a church procedure (rather than, or in addition to, a legal procedure), you should consult your priest or minister.

A divorce is generally easier to get than an annulment. This is because all you need to prove to get a divorce is that your marriage is broken.

How do you prove this? Simply by saying it. The PETITION FOR DIVORCE (Forms 4, 5, 6, 7, and 8), reads: "The marriage has become insupportable because of discord or conflict of personalities between the parties that destroys the legitimate ends of the marriage relationship and prevents any reasonable expectation of reconciliation." That is all you need to do. However, in order to get an annulment you'll need to prove more. This proof will involve introducing various documents into evidence, and having other people come to testify at the court hearing.

GROUNDS FOR
ANNULMENT

Annulments can only be granted under one of the following circumstances:

1. One of the parties was too young to get married. In Texas, both parties must be at least eighteen years old to get married, unless the underage person has parental consent and is at least fourteen.

2. If one of the parties is guilty of fraud. For example, where one party just got married in order to have the right to inherit from the other, with no intention of ever living together as husband and wife.

3. If one party was under duress when he or she got married. *Duress* means that the person was being threatened, or was under some kind of pressure, so that he or she did not get married voluntarily.

4. If one party didn't have the mental capacity to get married. This means the person was suffering from mental illness or mental disability (such as being severely retarded) to such an extent that the person didn't understand he or she was getting married; or possibly didn't even understand the concept of marriage.

5. If one party was already married to another person. This might occur if one party married, mistakenly believing the divorce from his or her previous spouse was final.

6. If the marriage is incestuous. Texas law prohibits marriage between certain family members, such as brother and sister, aunt and nephew, or uncle and niece.

7. If one party was under the influence of alcohol or narcotics at the time of the marriage.

8. If one party, for physical or mental reasons, was permanently impotent at the time of the marriage and did not inform the other party of the impotency.

9. If one party was divorced within thirty days of the marriage and did not inform the other party of the divorce or the other party could not have reasonably discovered the divorce.

10. If the marriage ceremony took place within seventy-two hours of the issuance of the marriage license.

If your spouse wants to stop an annulment, there are several arguments he or she could make to further complicate the case. There are no Texas Statutes outlining the proper procedures to follow to obtain an annulment (although many of the procedures governing a suit for divorce apply to a suit for an annulment), and annulments are much less common than divorces. The annulment procedure can be extremely complicated, and should not be attempted without consulting a lawyer.

LEGAL SEPARATION

Texas does not permit a *legal separation*. This procedure is available in some states, and is used to divide the property and provide for child support in cases where the husband and wife live separately, but remain married. This was usually used to break the financial rights and obligations of a couple whose religion did not permit divorce. Some states refer to this procedure as *divorce from bed and board*. It is an old procedure that is gradually fading out. However, it is possible to obtain support without getting a divorce, but that procedure is beyond the scope of this book.

THE LEGAL SYSTEM 2

This chapter will give you a general introduction to the legal system. There are things you need to know in order to obtain a divorce (or help your lawyer get the job done), and to get through any encounter with the legal system with a minimum of stress. These are some of the realities of our system. If you don't learn to accept these realities, you will experience much stress and frustration.

THEORY VS. REALITY

Our legal system is a system of rules. There are basically three types of rules:

1. Rules of Law: These are the basic substance of the law, such as a law telling a judge how to go about dividing your property.

2. Rules of Procedure: These outline how matters are to be handled in the courts, such as requiring court papers to be in a certain form, or filed within a certain time.

3. Rules of Evidence: These set forth the manner in which facts are to be proven.

The theory is that these rules allow each side to present evidence most favorable to that side, and an independent person or persons (the judge or jury) will be able to figure out the truth. Then certain legal principles will be applied to that "truth" which will give a fair resolution of the dispute between the parties. These legal principles are supposed to be relatively unchanging so that we can all know what will happen in any given situation and can plan our lives accordingly. This will provide order and predictability to our society. Any change in the legal principles is supposed to occur slowly, so that the expected behavior in our society is not confused from day-to-day. Unfortunately, the system does not really work this way. What follows are only some of the problems in the real legal system.

The system is not perfect. Contrary to how it may seem, legal rules are not made just to complicate the system and confuse everyone. They are attempts to make the system as fair and just as possible. They have been developed over several hundred years, and in most cases they do make sense. Unfortunately, our efforts to find fairness and justice have resulted in a complex set of rules. The legal system affects our lives in important ways, and it is not a game. However, it can be compared to a game in some ways. The rules are designed to apply to all people, in all cases. Sometimes the rules don't seem to give a fair result in a certain situation, but the rules are still followed. Just as a referee can make a bad call, so can a judge. There are also cases where one side wins by cheating.

Judges don't always follow the rules. This is a shocking discovery for many young lawyers. After spending three years in law school learning legal theory, and after spending countless hours preparing for a hearing and having all of the law on your side, you find that the judge isn't going to pay any attention to legal theories and the law. Many judges are going to make a decision simply on what they think seems fair under the circumstances. This concept is actually being taught in some law schools now. Unfortunately, what "seems fair" to a particular judge may depend upon his personal ideas and philosophy. For example, there is nothing in the divorce laws that gives one parent priority in child custody; however, a vast majority of judges believe that a child is generally better off with its mother. All other things being equal, these judges will find a way to justify awarding custody to the mother. There are many fine, intelligent, and legally correct judges. But there are also many that can make you wonder how they managed to graduate from high school!

The system is often slow. Even lawyers get frustrated at how long it can take to get a case completed (especially if they don't get paid until it's done). Whatever your situation, things will take longer than you expect. Patience is required to get through the system with a minimum of stress. Don't let your impatience or frustration show. No matter what happens, keep calm and be courteous. Be polite: to the judge, to the court clerks, to any lawyers involved, and even to your spouse. However, if you and your spouse can agree on everything, it is possible to complete the divorce process in about three weeks.

No two cases are alike. Just because your friend's case went a certain way doesn't mean yours will have the same result. The judge can make a difference, and more often the circumstances will make a difference. Just because your co-worker makes the same income as you and has the same number of children, you can't assume you will be ordered to pay the same amount of child support. There are usually other circumstances your co-worker doesn't tell you about, and possibly doesn't understand.

Half of the people "lose." Remember, there are two sides to every legal issue, and there is usually only one winner. Don't expect to have every detail go your way. If you leave anything to the judge to decide, you can expect to have some things go your spouse's way.

DIVORCE LAW AND PROCEDURE

This section will give you a general overview of the law and procedures involved in getting a divorce. To most people, including lawyers, the law appears very complicated and confusing. Fortunately, many areas of the law can be broken down into simple and logical steps. Divorce is one of those areas. Law and the legal system are often compared to games, and just like games, it is important to know the players.

The judge. The judge has the power to decide whether you can get divorced, how your property will be divided, which of you will get custody of the children, and how much the other will pay for child support. The judge is the last person you want to anger! In general, judges have large caseloads and like it best when your case can be concluded quickly and without hassle. This means that the more you and your spouse agree upon, and the more complete your paperwork is, the better the judge will like it. Most likely, your only direct contact with the judge will be at the final hearing, which may last as little as five minutes. (See the section on COURTROOM MANNERS in chapter 6 for more about how to deal with the judge.)

The judge's secretary. The judge's secretary sets the hearings for the judge and can frequently answer many of your questions about the procedure and what the judge would like or require. Once again, you don't want to make an enemy of the secretary. This means that you don't call him or her often, and don't ask too many questions. A few questions are okay, and you may want to start off saying that you just want to make sure you have everything in order for the judge. Be friendly and courteous, even if the secretary is rude. The judge's secretary has a large caseload just like the judge, and may be suffering from stress; or may just be a nasty person. However, you'll get farther by being nice than by arguing with or complaining to him or her.

The court clerk. Where the secretary usually only works for one judge, the court clerk handles the files for all of the judges. The clerk's office is the central place where all of the court files are kept. The clerk files your court papers and keeps the official records of your divorce. Most people who work in the clerk's office are friendly and helpful. While they can't give you legal advice (such as telling you what to say in your court papers), they can help explain the system and the procedures (such as telling you what type of papers must be filed). The clerk has the power to accept or reject your papers, so you don't want to anger the clerk either. If the clerk tells you to change something in your papers, just change it. Don't argue or complain.

If you anger the judge, his or her secretary, or the clerk, any one of them can delay your divorce or cause you a number of problems. So be polite, courteous and friendly to all of these people. It never hurts to engage in a little small talk, or to express your sympathy or understanding for all of the rude people they have to deal with and with their heavy workload.

Lawyers. Lawyers serve as guides through the legal system. They try to guide their own client while trying to confuse, manipulate, or out-maneuver their opponent. In dealing with your spouse's lawyer (if he or she has one) try to be polite. You won't get anywhere by being antagonistic or by arguing. Generally, the lawyer is just doing his or her job by trying to get the best situation for the client. Some lawyers are truly nasty people who can't deal with their opponent on a civilized basis. These lawyers simply can't be reasoned with, and you shouldn't try. If your spouse gets one of these lawyers, it may be a good idea for you to get a lawyer also. A lawyer can sometimes get you through the legal system faster, while helping you avoid the "dangers" along the way. Chapter 3 will provide more information about whether you need a lawyer.

This book. This book will serve as your guide throught the court system. In most cases, the dangers along the way are relatively small. If you were on trial for a crime, or for seriously injuring someone, there is no question that you would need a lawyer. But that's not the case with seeking a divorce. And if you start getting lost, or the dangers seem to be getting worse, you can always hire a lawyer to jump to your aid.

THE LAW   The law relating to divorce, as well as to any other area of law, comes from two sources. The first source is the *Texas Statutes*, which are the laws passed by the Texas Legislature. This book is designed so that you won't need to look up the law.

> **Residency Requirement**: Two basic laws you need to be aware of are that either you or your spouse must live in Texas for at least six months immediately before filing a petition with the court, and you must be a resident of the county in which you file the PETITION FOR DIVORCE for at least ninety days before filing the petition.

The other source of law is the past decisions of the Texas courts. These are much more difficult to locate and follow. For most situations the law is clearly spelled out in the statutes, and the past court decisions are not all that important. However, if you wish to learn more about how to find these court decisions, see the section on LEGAL RESEARCH later in this chapter.

The law is really very simple in most divorce cases. You will need to show the following three things:

1. That your marriage has become "insupportable." (This is done simply by stating this fact, which means that your marriage relationship is broken and can't be saved).

2. How your property should be divided between you and your spouse.

3. Who should have custody of your children, if any, and how they should be supported.

THE PROCEDURE

The basic uncontested divorce process may be viewed as a five-step process:

1. File court papers asking the judge to grant a divorce (which includes dividing your property and deciding how the children will be taken care of).

2. Notify your spouse that you are filing for divorce.

3. File papers explaining what you and your spouse have agreed upon with regard to property division and child custody.

4. Obtain a hearing date.

5. Attend a hearing with the judge, and have the judge sign a decree granting the divorce.

Now we'll look at these steps in a little more detail, and later chapters will tell you how to carry out these steps.

Petition for divorce. This is nothing more than a written request for the judge to grant you a divorce, divide your property, and determine child support and custody. Petition forms are provided in appendix B of this book, and full instructions are also provided in later chapters. Once the Petition is completed, it is taken to the court clerk to be filed.

Notifying your spouse. After you've prepared the petition you need to officially notify your spouse. Even though your spouse may already know that you are filing for divorce, you still need to have him or her officially notified. This is done by having a copy of your petition delivered to your spouse. This may be done in various ways, which will be explained in detail later.

Obtaining a hearing date. Once all of your paperwork is in order and has been filed, you need to set a date for a hearing. A hearing is simply a meeting with the judge so that he or she can give you a divorce. This is usually done by the court clerk when you file your petition.

The hearing. Finally, you go to the hearing. The judge will review the papers you have submitted, and any additional information you have, and will make a decision about whether to grant the divorce, how your property should be divided, who should have custody of your children, and how the children are to be supported. If you and your spouse agree on these matters, the judge will simply approve your agreement.

The judge can order the husband and wife into mediation when the parties are having a difficult time reaching agreement on the major issues. Also, marriage counseling can be ordered if the judge has reason to believe that the marriage can be saved; however, this is an extremely rare situation. The judge can also direct the state Department of Human Resources to conduct a study and provide the judge with a custody recommendation.

LEGAL RESEARCH

This book has been designed so that you don't need to do legal research. However, if your case becomes complicated, or you simply have an interest in checking into the divorce law in Texas, this section will give you some guidance.

TEXAS
STATUTES AND
CODES

The main source of information on Texas divorce law is the Texas statutes and codes. This is a set of volumes that contain the laws passed by the Texas Legislature. Some volumes are labelled "Statutes" and other are labelled "Codes." Supplements are issued each year. A set can usually be found at the public library, although check to be sure they have the most recent set. You will primarily be concerned with chapter 6 of the Family Code contained within the Texas statutes and codes, although you can look for other subjects in the index volume.

In addition to the laws passed by the legislature, law is also made by the decisions of the judges in various cases each year. To find this *case law* you will need to go to a law library. Each county has a law library connected with the court, so you can ask the court clerk where the library is located. Also, law schools have libraries that may be open to the public. Don't be afraid to ask the librarian for assistance. They cannot give you legal advice, but they can tell you where the books are located and they might even be kind enough to give you a short course on legal research. There are several types of books used to find the case law:

TEXAS
STATUTES AND
CODES
ANNOTATED

The *Texas Statutes Annotated* and the *Texas Codes Annotated* are numerous volumes that contain the Texas Statutes and Texas Codes, followed by summaries (or *annotations*) of court cases which discuss each section of the statutes. For example, if you are looking for information about division of property, you would find Section 7.001 of the Texas Family

Code. This would give you the exact language of the statute, which would be followed by summaries of court opinions explaining the alimony statute.

TEXAS DIGEST

The *Texas Digest* is a set of volumes that give short summaries of cases, and the place where you can find the court's full written opinion. The information in the digest is arranged alphabetically by subject. Find the chapter on "Divorce," then look for the headings of the subject you want.

SOUTHWESTERN REPORTER

The *Southwestern Reporter* is where the appeals courts publish their written opinions on the cases they hear. There are two "series" of the *Southwestern Reporter*, the older cases being found in the *Southwestern Reporter* (abbreviated "S.W."), and newer cases being found in the *Southwestern Reporter 2d Series* (abbreviated "S.W.2d"). For example, if the digest tells you that the case of *Woody v. Woody* is located at "371 S.W.2d 576," you can find the case by going to Volume 371 of the *Southwestern Reporter 2d Series*, and turning to page 576. In its opinion, the court will discuss what the case was about, what questions of law were presented for consideration, and what the court decided and why.

TEXAS JURISPRUDENCE

Texas Jurisprudence is a legal encyclopedia. You simply look up the subject you want ("Family Law/Dissolution of Marriage"), in alphabetical order, and it gives you a summary of the law on that subject. It will also refer to specific court cases, which can then be found in the *Southwestern Reporter*. Texas Jurisprudence deals specifically with Texas cases. There are also more general legal encyclopedias that cover the entire United States. These are *American Jurisprudence* (abbreviated "Am.Jur." and "Am.Jur. 2d") and *Corpus Juris Secundum* (abbreviated "C.J.S.").

TEXAS RULES OF COURT

The *Texas Rules of Court* are the rules that are applied in the various courts in Texas, and they also contain some approved forms. These rules mainly deal with forms and procedures. You would be primarily concerned with the "Rules of Civil Procedure."

OTHER
SOURCES

Three books you may want to ask for at the law library are: *Family Law Practice Manual*, by the Family Law Section of the State Bar of Texas; *Texas Family Law*, by Loy M. Simpkins; and *O'Conner's Texas Rules—Civil Trial*, by Texas Lawyer.

LAWYERS 3

Whether or not you need an attorney will depend upon many factors, such as how comfortable you feel handling the matter yourself, whether your situation is more complicated than usual, how much opposition you get from your spouse, and whether your spouse has an attorney. It may also be advisable to hire an attorney if you encounter a judge with a hostile attitude, or if your spouse gets a lawyer who wants to fight. There are no court appointed lawyers in divorce cases, so if you want an attorney you will have to hire one.

A very general rule is that you should consider hiring an attorney whenever you reach a point where you no longer feel comfortable representing yourself. This point will vary greatly with each person, so there is no easy way to be more definite.

A more appropriate question is: "Do you want a lawyer?" The next section will discuss some of the "pros" and "cons" of hiring a lawyer, and some of the things you may want to consider in making this decision.

DO YOU WANT A LAWYER?

One of the first questions you will want to consider, and most likely the reason you are reading this book, is: How much will an attorney cost?

Attorneys come in all ages, shapes, sizes, sexes, racial and ethnic groups—and price ranges. For a very rough estimate, you can expect an attorney to charge anywhere from $150 to $1,000 for an uncontested divorce, and from $800 and up for a contested divorce. Lawyers usually charge an hourly rate for contested divorces, ranging from about $75 to $300 per hour. Most new (and therefore less expensive) attorneys would be quite capable of handling a simple divorce, but, if your situation became more complicated, you would probably prefer a more experienced lawyer.

ADVANTAGES TO
HIRING A
LAWYER

Some advantages to hiring a lawyer include:

☞ Judges and other attorneys may take you more seriously if you have an attorney represent you. Most judges prefer both parties to have attorneys. They feel this helps the case move in a more orderly fashion because both sides will know the procedures and relevant issues. Persons representing themselves very often waste a lot of time on matters that have absolutely no bearing on the outcome of the case.

☞ A lawyer will serve as a "buffer" between you and your spouse. This can lead to a quicker passage through the system by reducing the chance for emotions to take control and confuse the issues.

☞ Attorneys prefer to deal with other attorneys for the same reasons listed above. However, if you become familiar with this book, and conduct yourself in a calm and proper manner, you should have no trouble. (Proper courtroom manners will be discussed in a later chapter.)

☞ You can let your lawyer worry about all of the details. By having an attorney you need only become generally familiar with the contents of this book, as it will be your attorney's job to file the proper papers in the correct form, and to deal with the court clerk, the judge, the process server, your spouse, and your spouse's attorney.

☞ Lawyers provide professional assistance with problems. In the event your case is complicated, or suddenly becomes complicated, it is an advantage to have an attorney who is familiar with your case. It can also be comforting to have a lawyer to turn to for advice, and to get your questions answered.

ADVANTAGES TO REPRESENTING YOURSELF

Some advantages to representing yourself include:

☞ Sometimes judges feel more sympathetic toward a person not represented by an attorney. Sometimes this results in the unrepresented person being allowed a certain amount of leeway with the procedure rules.

☞ The procedure may be faster. Two of the most frequent complaints about lawyers received by the bar association involve delay in completing the case, and failure to return phone calls. Most lawyers have a heavy caseload, which sometimes results in cases being neglected for various periods of time. If you are following the progress of your own case you'll be able to push it along the system diligently.

☞ Selecting any attorney is not easy. As the next section shows, it is hard to know whether you are selecting an attorney you will be happy with.

MIDDLE GROUND

You may want to look for an attorney who will be willing to accept an hourly fee to answer your questions and give you help as you need it. This way you will save some legal costs, but still get professional assistance.

SELECTING A LAWYER

Selecting a lawyer is a two-step process. First you need to decide which attorney to make an appointment with, then you need to decide if you want to hire that attorney.

FINDING A
LAWYER

There are several ways to go about finding a lawyer, including:

☞ Ask a friend. A common, and frequently the best, way to find a lawyer is to ask someone you know to recommend one to you. This is especially helpful if the lawyer represented your friend in a divorce or other family law matter.

☞ Lawyer Referral Service. You can find a referral service by looking in the Yellow Pages phone directory under "Attorney Referral Services" or "Attorneys." This is a service, usually operated by a bar association, which is designed to match a client with an attorney handling cases in the area of law the client needs. The referral service does not guarantee the quality of work, nor the level of experience or ability, of the attorney. Finding a lawyer this way will at least connect you with one who is interested in divorce and family law matters, and probably has some experience in this area.

☞ Yellow Pages. Check under the heading for "Attorneys" in the Yellow Pages phone directory. Many of the lawyers and law firms will place display ads here indicating their areas of practice and educational backgrounds. Look for firms or lawyers that indicate they practice in areas such as "divorce," "family law," or "domestic relations."

☞ Ask another lawyer. If you have used the services of an attorney in the past for some other matter (for example, a real estate closing, traffic ticket, or a will), you may want to call and ask if he or she could refer you to an attorney whose ability in the area of family law is respected.

EVALUATING A
LAWYER

From your search you should select three to five lawyers worthy of further consideration. Your first step will be to call each attorney's office, explain that you are interested in seeking a divorce, and ask the following questions:

☞ Does the attorney (or firm) handle this type of matter?

☛ How much can you expect it to cost? (Don't expect to get much of an answer.)

☛ How soon can you get an appointment?

If you like the answers you get, ask if you can speak to the attorney. Some offices will permit this, but others will require you to make an appointment. Make the appointment if that is what is required. Once you get in contact with the attorney (either on the phone or at the appointment), ask the following questions:

☛ How much will it cost?

☛ How will the fee be paid?

☛ How long has the attorney been in practice?

☛ How long has the attorney been in practice in Texas?

☛ What percentage of the attorney's cases involve divorce cases or other family law matters? (Don't expect an exact answer, but you should get a rough estimate that is at least twenty percent.)

☛ How long will it take? (Don't expect an exact answer, but the attorney should be able to give you an average range and discuss things which may make a difference.)

If you get acceptable answers to these questions, it's time to ask yourself the following questions about the lawyer:

☛ Do you feel comfortable talking to the lawyer?

☛ Is the lawyer friendly toward you?

☛ Does the lawyer seem confident in himself or herself?

☛ Does the lawyer seem to be straightforward with you, and able to explain things so you understand?

If you get satisfactory answers to all of these questions you probably have a lawyer you'll be able to work with. Most clients are happiest with an attorney they feel comfortable with.

WORKING WITH A LAWYER

In general, you will work best with your attorney if you keep an open, honest, and friendly attitude. You should also consider the following suggestions.

Ask questions. If you want to know something or if you don't understand something, ask your attorney. If you don't understand the answer, tell your attorney and ask him or her to explain it again. There are many points of law that many lawyers don't even fully understand, so you shouldn't be embarrassed to ask questions. Many people who say they had a bad experience with a lawyer either didn't ask enough questions, or had a lawyer who wouldn't take the time to explain things to them. If your lawyer isn't taking the time to explain what he or she is doing, it may be time to look for a new lawyer.

Give your lawyer complete information. Anything you tell your attorney is confidential. An attorney can lose his license to practice if he or she reveals information without your permission, so don't hold back. Tell your lawyer everything, even if it doesn't seem important to you. There are many things that seem unimportant to a non-attorney, but can change the outcome of a case. Also, don't hold something back because you are afraid it will hurt your case. It will definitely hurt your case if your lawyer doesn't find out about it until he or she hears it in court from your spouse's attorney! But if your lawyer knows in advance, he or she can plan to eliminate or reduce damage to your case.

Accept reality. Listen to what your lawyer tells you about the law and the system. It will do you no good to argue because the law or the system doesn't work the way you think it should. For example, if your lawyer tells you that the judge can't hear your case for two weeks, don't try demanding that he or she set a hearing tomorrow. By refusing to accept reality, you are only setting yourself up for disappointment. And remember: It's not your attorney's fault that the system isn't perfect or that the law doesn't say what you'd like it to say.

Be patient. This applies to being patient with the system (which is often slow, as we discussed earlier), as well as with your attorney. Don't expect your lawyer to return your phone call within an hour. Your lawyer may not be able to return you call the same day either. Most lawyers are very busy, and often overworked. It is rare that an attorney can maintain a full caseload and still make each client feel as if he or she is the only client.

Talk to the secretary. Your lawyer's secretary can be a valuable source of information, so be friendly and get to know him or her. Often the secretary will be able to answer your questions, and you won't get a bill for this time.

Let your attorney deal with your spouse. It is your lawyer's job to communicate with your spouse, or with your spouse's lawyer. Let your lawyer do his or her job. Many lawyers have had clients lose or damage their cases when the client decides to say or do something on their own.

Be on time. This applies to appointments with your lawyer, and to court hearings.

Keeping your case moving. Many lawyers operate on the old principle of the squeaking wheel gets the oil. Work on a case tends to get put off until a deadline is near, an emergency develops, or the client calls. There is a reason for this. Many lawyers take more cases than can be effectively handled in order to earn the income they desire. Your task is to become a squeaking wheel that doesn't squeak so much as to become annoying. Whenever you talk to your lawyer ask the following questions:

- ☞ What is the next step?

- ☞ When do you expect it to be done?

- ☞ When should I talk to you next?

If you don't hear from the lawyer when you expect, call him or her the following day. Don't remind your lawyer that he or she didn't call; just ask how things are going.

How to save money. Of course you don't want to spend unnecessary money for an attorney. Here are a few things you can do to avoid excess legal fees:

- ☞ Don't make unnecessary phone calls to your lawyer.

- ☞ Give information to the secretary whenever possible.

- ☞ Direct your question to the secretary first. She or he will refer your question to the attorney if necessary.

- ☞ Plan your phone calls so you can get to the point, and take less of your attorney's time.

- ☞ Do some of the "leg work" yourself. Pick up and deliver papers yourself, for example. Ask your attorney what you can do to assist with your case.

- ☞ Be prepared for appointments. Have all related papers with you, plan your visit to get to the point, and make an outline of what you want to discuss and what questions you want to ask.

Pay your attorney bill when it's due. No client gets prompt attention like a client who pays his or her lawyer on time. However, you are entitled to an itemized bill, showing what the attorney did and how much time it took. Many attorneys will have you sign an agreement that states how you will be charged, what is included in the hourly fee, and what is extra. Review your bill carefully. There are numerous stories of people paying an attorney $500 or $1,000 in advance, only to have the attorney make a few phone calls to the spouse's lawyer, then ask for more money. If your attorney asks for $500 or $1,000 in advance, you should be sure that you and the lawyer agree on what is to be done for this fee. For $500 you should at least expect to have a petition prepared, filed with the court, and served on your spouse (although the filing and service fees will probably be extra).

Firing your lawyer. If you find that you can no longer work with your lawyer, or don't trust your lawyer, it is time to either go it alone or get a new attorney. You will need to send your lawyer a letter stating that you no longer desire his or her services, and are discharging him or her from your case. Also state that you will be coming by his or her office the following day to pick up your file. The attorney does not have to give you his or her own notes or other work in progress, but he or she must give you the essential contents of your file (such as copies of papers already filed or prepared and billed for, and any documents you provided). If your attorney refuses to give you your file, for any reason, contact the Texas Bar Association about filing a complaint or *grievance* against the lawyer. Of course, you will need to settle any remaining fees charges.

DO YOU REALLY WANT A DIVORCE? 4

Getting a divorce is one of the most emotionally stressful events in a person's life. Only the death of one's child or spouse creates more stress than a divorce. It will also have an impact on several aspects of your life, and can change your entire lifestyle. Before you begin the process of getting a divorce, you need to take some time to think about how it will affect your life. This chapter will help you examine these things, and offer alternatives in the event you want to try to save your relationship. Even if you feel absolutely sure that you want a divorce, you should still read this chapter so you are prepared for what may follow.

LEGAL DIVORCE

In emotional terms, the legal aspect is the easiest part of divorce. It is simply the breaking of your matrimonial bonds; the termination of your marriage contract and partnership. The stress created here is that of going through a court system procedure, and having to deal with your spouse as you go through it. However, when compared to the other aspects of divorce, the legal divorce doesn't last as long. On the other hand, the legal divorce can be the most confrontational and emotionally explosive stage.

There are generally three matters to be resolved through the legal divorce:

1. The divorce of two people: Basically, this gives each the legal right to marry someone else.

2. The division of their property (and responsibility for debts).

3. The care and custody of their children.

Although it is theoretically possible for the legal divorce to be concluded within a few months, the legalities most often continue for years. This is mostly caused by the emotional aspects leading to battles over the children.

SOCIAL AND EMOTIONAL DIVORCE

Divorce will have a tremendous impact on your social and emotional life, which will continue long after you are legally divorced. This impact includes:

Lack of companionship. Even if your relationship is quite stormy, you are probably still accustomed to having your spouse around. You may be able to temporarily put aside your problems, and at least somewhat support each other in times of mutual adversity (such as in dealing with a death in the family, the illness of your child, or hurricane damage to your home). You may also feel a little more secure at night knowing you are not alone in the house. Even if your marriage is one of the most miserable, you may still notice at least a little emptiness, loneliness, or solitude after the divorce. It may not be that you miss your spouse in particular, but just miss another person being around.

Grief. Divorce may be viewed as the death of a marriage, or maybe the funeral ceremony for the death of a marriage. And like the death of anyone or anything you've been close to, you will feel a sense of loss. This aspect can take you through all of the normal feelings associated with grief, such as guilt, anger, denial, and acceptance. You'll get angry and frustrated over the years you've "wasted." You'll feel guilty because you "failed to make the marriage work." You'll find yourself saying, "I can't believe this is happening to me." And, for months or even years, you'll spend a lot of time thinking about your marriage. It can be extremely difficult to put it all behind you, and to get on with your life.

The single's scene: dating. If you want to avoid solitary evenings before the TV, you'll find yourself trying to get back into the single's scene. This will probably involve a change in friends, as well as a change in lifestyle. First, you may find that your current friends, who are probably all married, no longer find that you, as a single person, fit in with their circle. Gradually, or even quickly, you may find yourself dropped from their guest list. Now, you've got to start making an effort to meet single people at work, going out on the town, and even dating! This experience can be very frightening, tiring, and frustrating after years of being away from this lifestyle. It can also be very difficult if you have custody of the kids. And the dating scene is (or at least should be) entirely changed with the ever-present threat of AIDS and other communicable diseases.

FINANCIAL DIVORCE

This can be a very long and drastic adjustment. Divorce has a significant financial impact in almost every case. Many married couples are just able to make ends meet. After getting divorced there are suddenly two rent payments, two electric bills, etc. For the spouse without custody, there is also child support to be paid. For at least one spouse, and often for both, money becomes even tighter than it was before the divorce. Also, once you've divided your property, each of you will need to replace the items the other person got to keep. If she got the bedroom furniture and the pots and pans, he will need to buy his own. If he got the TV and the sofa, she will need to buy her own TV and sofa.

CHILDREN AND DIVORCE

The effect upon your children, and your relationship with them, can be the most painful and long-lasting aspect of divorce. Your family life will be permanently changed, as there will no longer be the "family." Even if you remarry, step-parents rarely bring back that same family feeling. Your relationship with your children may become strained as they work through their feelings of blame, guilt, disappointment, and anger. This strain may continue for many years. Your children may even need professional counseling. Also, as long as there is child support and visitation involved, you will be forced to have at least some contact with your ex-spouse.

ALTERNATIVES TO DIVORCE

By the time you've purchased this book, and read this far, you have probably already decided that you want a divorce. However, if what you've just read and thought about has changed your mind, or made you want to make a last effort to save your marriage, there are a few things you can try. These are only very basic suggestions. Details, and other suggestions, can be offered by professional marriage counselors.

TALK TO YOUR SPOUSE
Choose the right time (not when your spouse is trying to unwind after a day at work, or is trying to quiet a screaming baby), and talk about your problems. Try to establish a few ground rules for the discussion, such as:

☞ Talk about how you feel, instead of making accusations that may start an argument.

☞ Each person listens while the other speaks (no interrupting).

☞ Each person must say something that he or she likes about the other, and about the relationship.

As you talk you may want to discuss such things as where you'd like your relationship to go, how it has changed since you got married, and what can be done to bring you closer together.

CHANGE YOUR THINKING

Many people get divorced because they won't change something about their outlook or their lifestyle. Then, once they get divorced, they find they've made that same change they resisted for so long.

For example, George and Wendy were unhappy in their marriage. They didn't seem to share the same lifestyle. George felt overburdened with responsibility, and bored. He wanted Wendy to be more independent and outgoing, to meet new people, to handle the household budget, and to go out with him more often. But Wendy was more shy and reserved, wasn't confident in her ability to find a job and succeed in the business world, and preferred to stay at home. Wendy wanted George to give up some of his frequent nights "out with the guys," to help with the cooking and laundry, to stop leaving messes for her to clean up, and to stop bothering her about going out all the time. But neither would try change, and eventually all of the "little things" built up into a divorce.

After the divorce, Wendy was forced to get a job to support herself. Now she's made friends at work, she goes out with them two or three nights a week, she's successful and happy at her job, and she's quite competent at managing her own budget. George now has his own apartment, and has to cook his own meals (something he finds he enjoys) and do his own laundry. He's also found it necessary to clean up his own messes and keep the place neat, especially if he's going to entertain guests. George has even thought about inviting Wendy over for dinner and a quiet evening at his place. Wendy has been thinking about inviting George out for a drink after work with her friends.

Both George and Wendy have changed in exactly the way the other had wanted. It's just too bad they didn't make these changes before they got divorced! If you think some change may help, give it a try. You can always go back to a divorce if things don't work out.

COUNSELING

Counseling is not the same as giving advice. A counselor should not be telling you what to do. A counselor's job is to assist you in figuring out what you really want to do. A counselor's job is mostly to ask questions that will get you thinking.

Actually, just talking things out with your spouse is a form of self-counseling. The only problem is that it's difficult to remain objective and non-judgmental. You both need to be able to calmly analyze what the problems are, and discuss possible solutions.

Very few couples seem to be able to do this successfully, which is why there are professional marriage counselors. As with doctors and lawyers, good marriage counselors are best discovered by word of mouth. You may have friends who can direct you to someone who helped them. You can also check with your family doctor or your clergyman for a referral, or even check the telephone Yellow Pages under "Marriage and Family Counselors" or some similar category. You can see a counselor either alone or with your spouse. It may be a good idea to see a counselor even if you are going through with the divorce. Another form of individual counseling is talking to a close friend. Just remember the difference between counseling and advice giving! Don't let your friend tell you what you should do.

TRIAL
SEPARATION

Before going through the time, expense, and trouble of getting a divorce, you and your spouse may want to try just getting away from each other for awhile. This can be as simple as taking separate vacations, or as complex as actually separating into separate households for an indefinite period of time.

This may give each of you a chance to think about how you'll like living alone, how important or trivial your problems are, and how you really feel about each other.

EVALUATING YOUR SITUATION 5

The following things should be done or considered before you begin the divorce process.

YOUR SPOUSE

First, you need to evaluate your situation with respect to your spouse. Have you both already agreed to get a divorce? If not, what kind of reaction do you expect from him or her? Your expected reaction can determine how you proceed. If he or she reacts in a rational manner, you can probably use the simplified or uncontested procedure. But, if you expect an extremely emotional and possibly violent reaction, you will need to take steps to protect yourself, your children, and your property, and will have to start out expecting to use the contested procedure.

You were warned on the back cover of this book not to let your spouse find this book, and it was for a very good reason. Unless you and your spouse have already decided together to get a divorce, you don't want your spouse to know you are thinking about filing for divorce. This is a defense tactic, although it may not seem that way at first. If your spouse thinks you are planning a divorce, he or she may do things to prevent you from getting a fair result. These things include withdrawing money from bank accounts, hiding information about income, and hiding assets. So don't let on until you've collected all of the information you will need and are about to file with the court, or until you are prepared to protect yourself from violence, if necessary.

> **Caution:** Tactics such as withdrawing money from bank accounts and hiding assets are dangerous. If you try any of these things you risk looking like the "bad guy" before the judge. This can result in anything from having disputed matters resolved in your spouse's favor, to being ordered to produce the assets (or be jailed for contempt of court).

Theoretically, the "system" would prefer you to keep evidence of the assets (such as photographs, sales receipts, or bank statements) to present to the judge if your spouse hides them. Then, your spouse will be the bad guy and risk being jailed. However, once your spouse has taken assets, and hidden them, or sold them and spent the money, even a contempt order may not get the money or assets back. If you determine that you need to get the assets in order to keep your spouse from hiding or disposing of them, be sure you keep them in a safe place. Do not dispose of them. If your spouse claims you took them, you can explain to the judge why you were afraid that your spouse would dispose of them and that you merely got them out of his or her reach.

GATHERING INFORMATION

It is extremely important that you collect all of the financial information you can get. This information should include originals or copies of the following:

1. Your most recent income tax return (and your spouse's if you filed separately).

2. The most recent W-2 tax forms for yourself and your spouse.

3. Any other income reporting papers (such as interest, stock dividends, etc.).

4. Your spouse's most recent paystub, hopefully showing year-to-date earnings (otherwise try to get copies of all paystubs since the beginning of the year).

5. Deeds to real estate; and titles to cars, boats, or other vehicles.

6. Your and your spouse's will.

7. Life insurance policies.

8. Stocks, bonds, or other investment papers.

9. Pension or retirement fund papers and statements.

10. Health insurance card and papers.

11. Bank account or credit union statements.

12. Your spouse's social security number and driver's license number.

13. Names, addresses, and phone numbers of your spouse's employer, close friends, and family members.

14. Credit card statements, mortgage documents, and other credit and debt papers.

15. A list of vehicles, furniture, appliances, tools, etc., owned by you and your spouse. (See the next section in this chapter on PROPERTY AND DEBTS for forms and a detailed discussion of what to include.)

16. Copies of bills or receipts for recurring, regular expenses, such as electric, gas, or other utilities, car insurance, etc.

17. Copies of bills, receipts, insurance forms, or medical records for any unusual medical expenses (including for recurring or continuous medical conditions) for yourself, your spouse, or your children.

18. Any other papers showing what you and your spouse earn, own or owe.

Make copies of as many of these papers as possible and keep them in a safe and private place (where your spouse won't find them). Try to make copies of new papers as they come in, especially as you get close to filing court papers, and as you get close to a court hearing.

PROPERTY AND DEBTS

PROPERTY   This section is designed to help you get a rough idea of where things stand regarding the division of your property and to prepare you for completing the court papers you will need to file. The following sections will deal with the questions of your debts, and child support, custody and visitation. If you are still not sure whether you want a divorce, these sections may help you to decide.

Texas characterizes property possessed by either spouse during marriage as community property or separate property. *Separate property* is property owned by a spouse before marriage, property acquired during the marriage by gift or inheritance, and funds recovered by the spouse for personal injuries. All other property of the spouses is *community property*. Each spouse automatically owns one-half of the community property and generally is entitled to that one-half upon divorce.

This section basically assists you in completing the PROPERTY INVENTORY (Form 1 in appendix B of this book). This form is a list of all of your property, and key information about that property. You will notice that this form is divided into nine columns, designated as follows:

Column (1): You will check the box in this column if that piece of property is "separate" property. This is property that either you or your spouse acquired before you were married, or that was given to you or your spouse separately, or that was inherited by you or your spouse separately. It also includes money one of you received for a personal injury claim.

Column (2): In this column you will describe the property. A discussion regarding what information should go in this column will follow.

Column (3): This column is used to write in the serial number, account number, or other number that will help clearly identify that piece of property.

Column (4): This is for the current market value of the property.

Column (5): This will show how much money is owed on the property, if any.

Column (6): Subtract the balance owed from the value. This will show how much the property is worth to you (your *equity*).

Column (7): This column will show the current legal owner of the property. (H) designates the husband, (W) the wife, and (J) is for jointly owned property (in both of your names).

Column (8): This column will be checked for those pieces of property you expect the husband will keep.

Column (9): This column is for the property you expect the wife will keep.

Use columns (1) through (7) to list your property, including the following:

Cash. List the name of the bank, credit union, etc., and the account number, for each account. This includes savings and checking accounts, and certificates of deposit ("CDs"). The balance of each account should be listed in the columns entitled "VALUE" and "EQUITY." (Leave the "BALANCE OWED" column blank.) Make copies of the most recent bank statements for each account.

Stocks and bonds. All stocks, bonds, or other "paper investments" should be listed. Write down the number of shares and the name of the company or other organization that issued them. Also copy any notation such as "common" or "preferred" stock or shares. This information can be obtained from the stock certificate itself, or from a statement from the stock broker. Make a copy of the certificate or the statement.

Real estate. List each piece of property you and your spouse own. The description might include a street address for the property, a subdivision name and lot number, or anything that lets you know what piece of property you are referring to. There probably won't be an ID number, although you might use the county's tax number. Real estate (or any other property) may be in both of your names (joint), in your spouse's name alone, or in your name alone. The only way to know for sure is to look at the deed to the property. (If you can't find a copy of the deed, try to find mortgage papers or payment coupons, homeowners insurance papers, or a property tax assessment notice.) The owners of property are usually referred to on the deed as the *grantees*. In assigning a value to the property, consider the market value, which is how much you could probably sell the property for. This might be what similar houses in your neighborhood have sold for recently. You might also consider how much you paid for the property, or how much the property is insured for. *Do not* use the tax assessment value, as this is usually considerably lower than the market value.

Vehicles. This category includes cars, trucks, motor homes, recreational vehicles ("RVs"), motorcycles, boats, trailers, airplanes, and any other means of transportation for which the state requires a title and registration. Your description should include the following information (which can usually be found on the title or on the vehicle itself):

- ☞ Year it was made.

- ☞ Make: The name of the manufacturer, such as "Ford," "Honda," "Chris Craft," etc.

☛ Model: You know it's a Ford, but is it a Mustang, an LTD, or an Aerostar: The model may be a name, a number, a series of letters, or a combination of these.

☛ Serial Number: This is most likely found on the vehicle, as well as on the title or registration.

Make a copy of the title or registration. Regarding a value, you can go to the public library and ask to look at the blue book for cars, trucks, or whatever it is you're looking for. A *blue book* (which may actually be yellow, black, or any other color) gives the average values for used vehicles. Your librarian can help you find what you need. Another source is to look in the classified advertising section of a newspaper to see what similar vehicles are selling for. You might also try calling a dealer to see if they can give you a rough idea of the value. Be sure you take into consideration the condition of the vehicle.

Furniture. List all furniture as specifically as possible. You should include the type (such as sofa, coffee table, etc.), the color, and if you know it, the manufacturer, line name or the style. Furniture usually won't have a serial number, although if you find one be sure to write it on the list. Just estimate a value, unless you just know what it's worth.

Appliances, electronic equipment, and yard machines. This category includes such things as refrigerators, lawn mowers, and power tools. Again, estimate a value, unless you are familiar enough with them to simply "know" what they are worth. There are too many different makes, models, accessories and age factors to be able to figure out a value otherwise. These items will probably have a make, model, and serial number on them. You may have to look on the back, bottom, or other hidden place for the serial number, but try to find it.

Jewelry and other valuables. You don't need to list inexpensive, or costume jewelry. And you can plan on keeping your own personal watches, rings, etc. However, if you own an expensive piece you should include it in your list, along with an estimated value. Be sure to include silverware, original art, gold, coin collections, etc. Again, be as detailed and specific as possible.

Life insurance with cash surrender value. This is any life insurance policy which you may cash in or borrow against, and therefore has value. If you can't find a cash surrender value in the papers you have, you can call the insurance company and ask.

Other "big ticket" items. This is simply a general reference to anything of significant value that doesn't fit in one of the categories already discussed. Examples might be a portable spa, an above-ground swimming pool, golf clubs, guns, pool tables, camping or fishing equipment, farm animals, or machinery.

Pensions and military benefits. The division of pensions, and military and retirement benefits, can be a complicated matter. Whenever these types of benefits are involved, you will need to consult an attorney or a CPA to determine the value of the benefits and how they should be divided. Be sure to read the section in chapter 13 on pension plans.

What not to list. You will not need to list your clothing and other personal effects. Pots and pans, dishes, and cooking utensils ordinarily do not need to be listed, unless they have some unusually high value.

Once you have completed your list, go back through it and try to determine who should end up with each item. The ideal situation is for both you and your spouse to go through the list together, and divide things fairly. However, if this is not possible, you will need to offer a reasonable settlement to the judge. Consider each item, and make a checkmark in either column (8) or (9) to designate whether that item should go to the husband or wife. You may make the following assumptions:

- ☞ Your separate property will go to you.

- ☞ Your spouse's separate property will go to your spouse.

- ☞ You should get the items that only you use.

- ☞ Your spouse should get the items only used by your spouse.

☞ The remaining items should be divided, evening out the total value of all the community property, and taking into consideration who would really want that item.

To somewhat equally divide your property (we're only talking about marital property here), you first need to know the total value of your property. First of all, do not count the value of the separate items. Add the remaining amounts in the "EQUITY" column of the PROPERTY INVENTORY (Form 1), which will give you an approximate value of all community property.

When it comes time for the hearing, you and your spouse may be arguing over some or all of the items on your list. This is when you'll be glad that you made copies of the documents relating to the property on your list. Arguments over the value of property may need to be resolved by hiring appraisers to set a value; however, you'll have to pay the appraiser a fee. Dividing your property will be discussed further in later chapters.

DEBTS This section relates to the DEBT INVENTORY (Form 2 in appendix B of this book), which will list your debts. Although there are cases where, for example, the wife gets a car but the husband is ordered to make the payments, generally whoever gets the property also gets the debt owed on that property. This seems to be a fair arrangement in most cases. On Form 2, you will list each debt owed by you or your spouse. As with separate property, there is also *separate debt*. This is any debt incurred before you were married, that is yours alone. Form 2 contains a column for "S" debts, which should be checked for each separate debt. You will be responsible for your separate debts, and your spouse will be responsible for his or hers.

To complete the DEBT INVENTORY (Form 2), list each debt as follows:

Column (1): Check if this is a separate debt.

Column (2): Write in the name and address of the creditor (the bank, company or person to whom the debt is owed).

Column (3):   Write in the account, loan, or mortgage number.

Column (4):   Write in any notes to help identify what the loan was for (such as "Christmas gifts," "Vacation," etc.).

Column (5):   Write in the amount of the monthly payment.

Column (6):   Write in the balance still owed on the loan.

Column (7):   Write in the date (approximately) when the loan was made.

Column (8):   Note whether the account is in the husband's name (H), the wife's name (W), or jointly in both names (J).

Columns (9) & (10):   These columns note who will be responsible for the debt after the divorce. As with your property, each of you will keep your separate debts, and the remainder should be divided taking into consideration who will keep the property the loan was for and equally dividing the debt.

CHILD CUSTODY AND VISITATION

As with everything else in divorce, things are ideal when both parties can agree on the question of custody of the children. Generally the judge will accept any agreement you reach, provided it doesn't appear that your agreement will cause harm to your children.

In Texas, child custody is formally referred to in the statutes as "managing conservatorship." Throughout this book, "child custody" and "managing conservatorship" are used interchangeably and mean the same thing. In Texas, any divorce involving minor children is technically considered two separate legal matters: (1) a divorce and (2) a "suit affecting the parent-child relationship." These will be joined together in your petition, and will be discussed more in a later chapter.

With respect to child custody, the Texas law makes two significant statements:

> It is the policy of this state to assure that children will have frequent and continuing contact with parents who have shown the ability to act in the best interest of the child, to provide a stable environment for the child, and to encourage parents to share in the rights and responsibilities of raising their children after the parents have separated or dissolved their marriage.

> The court shall apply the [child custody] guidelines without regard to the sex of the parents or the child.

In spite of this modern philosophy voiced by the Texas courts and legislature, you will find that most judges are from the old school of thought on this subject and believe that (all things being equal) a young child is better off with the mother. Because of these statements in the law (mentioned above) the judge may go to great lengths to find that all things are not equal, so as to justify his or her decision to award custody to the mother. It happens day after day throughout the state, and it's a reality you may have to deal with.

The Texas law also states that the court may appoint the parents as joint managing conservators of the child in its decree only if the judge finds that the appointment of both parents is in the best interest of the child. This is commonly referred to as *joint custody*. To determine the best interest of the child, the judge will consider the following factors:

1. Whether the physical, psychological, or emotional needs and development of the child will benefit from the appointment of joint custodians.

2. The ability of the parents to put the welfare of the child first and reach agreement on what is in the child's best interest.

3. Whether each parent can encourage and accept a positive relationship between the child and the other parent.

4. Whether both parents took a role in raising the child prior to the divorce.

5. The physical distance between the homes of each parent.

6. The preference of a child twelve years of age or older with regard to joint custody.

7. Whether there is a history of family violence involving the parents of the child.

8. Any other factor the judge believes is relevant.

While joint custody is a great idea in its concept, it is usually not a very practical one. Very few parents can put aside their anger at each other to agree on what is best for their child. Joint custody merely leads to more fighting. And even if joint custody is ordered, a child can only have one primary residence. So the judge may still decide which parent the child will mainly live with, as well as how decisions regarding such things as education and medical and dental care will be made.

If you and your spouse cannot agree on how these matters will be handled, you will be leaving this important decision to the judge. The judge cannot possibly know your child as well as you and your spouse, so doesn't it make sense for you to work this out yourselves? Otherwise, you are leaving the decision to a stranger.

If the judge must decide the question of custody, he or she will consider the following factors:

☛ Which parent is most likely to allow the other to visit with the child.

- The love, affection, and other emotional ties existing between the child and each parent.

- The ability and willingness of each parent to provide the child with food, clothing, medical care, and other material needs.

- The length of time the child has lived with either parent in a stable environment.

- The permanence, as a family unit, of the proposed custodial home. (This relates to where one of the parties will be getting remarried immediately after the divorce or, more often, to change of custody petitions at a later date.)

- The moral fitness of each parent.

- The mental and physical health of each parent.

- The home, school, and community record of the child.

- The preference of the child, providing the child is of sufficient intelligence and understanding.

- Any other fact the judge decides is relevant.

It is difficult to predict the outcome of a custody battle. There are too many factors and individual circumstances to make such a guess. The only exception is where one parent is clearly unfit and the other can prove it. Drug abuse is probably the most common charge against a spouse, but unless there has been an arrest and conviction it is difficult to prove to a judge. In general, don't charge your spouse with being unfit unless you can prove it. Judges are not impressed with unfounded allegations, and they can do more harm that good.

In Texas, the law contains a model "standard possession order." (See Section 153.316 of the Family Code in appendix A of this book.) This sets forth the terms of visitation for the parent who does not have custody of the child. A typical standard possession order is included in appendix B as Form 22. This is the order that a judge will generally use to establish visitation rights if you and your spouse do not agree on other terms.

If your children are older (not infants), it may be a good idea to seriously consider their preference for with whom they would like to live. Your "fairness" and respect for their wishes may benefit you in the long run. Just be sure that you keep in close contact with them and visit them often.

CHILD SUPPORT

Once again, the judge will probably go along with any agreement you and your spouse reach, as long as he or she is satisfied that the child will be adequately taken care of. The following information and the CHILD SUPPORT GUIDELINES WORKSHEET (Form 3), will help you get an idea of the proper amount of child support. Form 3 consists of one main page, followed by Schedules A, B, C, and D. The schedules are used to help you complete the form. Here you are only trying to get a rough idea of the amount of child support to expect. Where an agreement cannot be reached the following procedure will be used:

HOW CHILD SUPPORT IS DETERMINED

Generally, there are two factors used to determine the proper amount of support to be paid: (1) the needs of the child, and (2) the financial ability of the parents to meet those needs. In Texas, the presumption is that the spouse who does not have physical custody of the child will be ordered to pay child support. This presumption assumes that the parent with custody will be spending resources of his or her own to provide shelter, food, etc. for the child.

The CHILD SUPPORT GUIDELINES WORKSHEET (Form 3) is simply to be used as a guideline for you to determine how much support would likely be ordered under the guidelines. The judge will take the following steps to determine the proper amount of support:

1. You and your spouse each provide proof of your gross income.

2. Taxes and other deductions are allowed to determine each of your "net resources."

3. The number of children you have is used to establish the percentage of net resources to be paid by the non-custodial parent (the *obligor*). This is done by reading the chart.

4. The net resources of the non-custodial parent (the obligor) are multiplied by the percentage obtained from the chart to arrive at the amount of support to be paid by the parent without custody.

Of course, if payment of child support would create an economic hardship on the obligor, and the custodial parent has sufficient resources to support the child, the judge may deviate from the guidelines and decrease the amount of child support to be paid by the obligor.

INCOME
DETERMINATION

Gross Income. The first thing you will need to do is determine your *gross income*. This is basically your income before any deductions for taxes, social security, etc. The following money sources are considered part of gross income:

☞ Gross salary or wages.

☞ Overtime, commissions, bonuses, allowances, tips, etc.

☞ Business income from self-employment, partnerships, corporations, and independent contracts (gross receipts, minus ordinary and necessary expenses).

☞ Disability benefits.

☞ Worker's compensation.

☞ Unemployment compensation.

☞ Pension, retirement, or annuity payments.

☞ Social security benefits.

☞ Alimony received from a previous marriage.

☞ Interest, dividends, and royalty income.

☞ Income from trusts or estates.

☞ Rental income (gross receipts, minus ordinary and necessary expenses—but not depreciation).

☞ Gains derived from dealings in property, unless the gain is nonrecurring.

☞ Reimbursed expenses to the extent they reduce living expenses (such as a rent allowance, or the value of an apartment provided by your employer).

These categories are all listed in Schedule A of Form 3. Fill in the amounts for yourself and your spouse in Schedule A. Then write in the totals on the line for STEP 1 of Form 3, which is on the first page of the form.

If you voluntarily reduce your income, or quit your job, the judge can refuse to recognize the reduction or loss of income. This is called *imputed income*, which is income you don't really have, but are considered capable of having. The only exception is where you are required to take such an action to stay home and care for your child. If this question comes up, the judge will decide whether you need to stay home, so be ready to explain your reasons.

Net Resources. Net resources are determined by subtracting certain deductions (listed in Schedule B) from your gross income. The following deductions are allowed:

☞ Federal income taxes. (The amount of the deduction will be based on withholding for a single person claiming one personal exemption and the standard deduction.)

☞ Social Security (FICA), or Self-Employment taxes.

☞ Mandatory union dues (where you must pay dues to keep your job).

☞ Health insurance payments for coverage of the child/children.

Fill in these deductions on Schedule B. Total the deductions, and write the totals on the line for STEP 2 on the first page of Form 3.

Your gross income minus these deductions will give your net resources. The same process should be used to determine your spouse's net resources. Write these figures in on the line for STEP 3 on the first page of Form 3.

CALCULATING
CHILD SUPPORT

Once you determine the obligor's net resources, turn to the child support guidelines table, which is Schedule C of Form 3 (this chart comes from Section 15 of the Texas Statutes). Simply find the number of children who will receive support and read across to get the percentage to be applied to the obligor's net resources. Multiply the obligor's net resources by this percentage and this will give you the amount of child support.

For example, if the obligor's net resources are $3,200 and there are two children who must be supported, the guideline amount of child support would be $800 per month ($3,200 x 25%).

There are several factors that may change the amount of child support ordered according to the guidelines explained above. The judge has the right to adjust the amount of support after taking into account the factors listed in Schedule D. You should review Schedule D to determine whether any of the items listed apply to your situation.

ALIMONY

Texas law has provided that temporary alimony, called *temporary support*, could be paid to a spouse after a PETITION FOR DIVORCE has been filed, and ending when the divorce becomes final. However, in order for temporary support to be ordered, it must be clearly shown that the spouse is in financial need of such support.

In 1995, the Texas legislature enacted statutes that permit a court to authorize the payment of post-divorce alimony, called *maintenance*. The basic requirements are as follows:

1. The parties must have been married at least ten years.

2. The party seeking maintenance either:

    a. lacks sufficient property to provide for his or her minimum needs because of an incapacitating physical or mental disability, or

    b. is the custodian of a child who requires care because of a physical or mental disability, or

    c. lacks the ability to earn sufficient income to provide a minimum level of support for himself or herself.

The amount of monthly maintenance cannot be more than $2,500.00 or twenty percent of the payor's income, whichever amount is less. Maintenance cannot be paid for longer than three years, and ends upon the death of either party or when the party receiving maintenance remarries.

A request for maintenance should be included in the original PETITION FOR DIVORCE.

GENERAL PROCEDURES **6**

AN INTRODUCTION TO LEGAL FORMS

The forms in this book are modeled after forms widely used by attorneys in Texas. Court clerks and judges are familiar with these forms and are not likely to object to them. The forms in this book are legally correct, however, one occasionally encounters a troublesome clerk or judge who is very particular about how he or she wants the forms. If you encounter any problem with the forms in this book being accepted by the clerk of judge, you can try one or more of the following:

☛ Ask the clerk or judge what is wrong with your form, then try to change it to suit the clerk or judge.

☛ Ask the clerk or judge if the local bar association has forms available. If forms are available, find out where you can get them, get them and use them. The instructions in this book will still help you to fill them out.

☛ Consult a lawyer.

Although the instructions in this book will tell you to "type in" certain information, it is not absolutely necessary to use a typewriter. If typing is not possible, you can print the information required in the forms. Just be sure your handwriting can be easily read, or the clerk may not accept your papers for filing.

Each form is referred to by both the title of the form and a form number. Be sure to check the form number because some of the forms have similar titles. The form number is found in the top outside corner of the first page of each form. Also, a list of the forms, by both number and name, is found at the beginning of appendix B.

You will notice that most of the forms in appendix B of this book have the same heading. The forms without this heading are not filed with the court, but are for your use only. The top portion of these court forms will all be completed in the same manner. The heading at the very top of the form tells which court your case is filed in. You will need to type in the number of the "judicial district" and the county in which the court is located. You can either look in the phone book, or call the court clerk's office to find out your court's district number.

Next, you need to type your full name, and your spouse's, on the lines at the left side of the form, below the words, "In the Matter of the Marriage of." Do not use nicknames or shortened versions of names. You should use the names as they appear on your marriage license, if possible. If you have minor children, include the words "And In the Interests Of" and type the names of the children.

You won't be able to type in a "Case Number" until after you file your petition with the clerk. The clerk will assign a case number and will write it on your petition and any other papers you file with it. You must include the case number on all papers you file later.

When completed, the top portion of your forms should look something like the example at the top of the following page.

NO. _____

IN THE MATTER OF
THE MARRIAGE OF   §   IN THE DISTRICT COURT
                                   §
                                   §
_____   §
                                   §
AND   §
                                   §
                                   §
_____   §   _____ JUDICIAL DISTRICT
                                   §
AND IN THE INTERESTS OF   §
                                   §
_____   §
                                   §
_____, and   §
                                   §
_____   §
MINOR CHILDREN   §   _____ COUNTY, TEXAS

FILING WITH THE COURT CLERK

Once you have decided which forms you need, and have them all prepared, it is time to file your case with the court clerk. First, make at least three copies of each form (the original for the clerk, one copy for yourself, one for your spouse, and one extra just in case the clerk asks for two copies or you decide to hire an attorney later).

Filing is actually about as simple as making a bank deposit, although the following information will help things go smoothly. Call the court clerk's office. You can find the phone number under the county government section of your phone directory. Ask the clerk the following questions (along with any other questions that come to mind, such as where the clerk's office is located and what their hours are):

☞   How much is the filing fee for a dissolution of marriage?

☞ Does the court have any special forms that need to be filed with the petition. (If there are special forms that do not appear in this book, then you will need to go down to the clerk's office and pick them up. There may be a fee, so ask.)

☞ How many copies of the petition and other forms do you need to file with the clerk?

Next, take your petition, and any other forms you determine you need, to the clerk's office. The clerk handles many different types of cases, so be sure to look for signs telling you which office or window to go to. You should be looking for signs that say such things as "Family Court," "Family Section," "Filing," etc. If it's too confusing, ask someone where you file a petition for divorce.

Once you've found the right place, simply hand the papers to the clerk and say, "I'd like to file this." The clerk will examine the papers, then do one of two things: either accept it for filing (and either collect the filing fee or direct you to where to pay it), or tell you that something is not correct. If you're told something is wrong, ask the clerk to explain to you what is wrong and how to correct the problem. Although clerks are not permitted to give legal advice, the types of problems they spot are usually very minor things that they can tell you how to correct. Often it is possible to figure out how to correct it from the way they explain what is wrong.

Notifying Your Spouse

If you and your spouse are in agreement about everything, you do not need to worry about the information in this section. Your spouse will sign a WAIVER OF CITATION (Form 10) and file this with the court. However, if you and your spouse are not in agreement, you are required to notify your spouse that you have filed for divorce. This gives your spouse a chance to respond to your petition. If you are unable to find your spouse, you will also need to read chapter 10.

NOTICE OF FILING THE PETITION

The usual way to notify your spouse that you filed for a divorce is called *personal service*, which is where the sheriff, or someone else designated by the judge, personally delivers the papers to your spouse.

Personal service is usually requested in the original petition. A separate paragraph is included in the petition and contains the residence or business address where you want service to be attempted on your spouse. The fee for personal service will be included in the original filing fee for the petition. When you ask the clerk for information about the filing fee for the petition, also ask what the additional fee is for personal service.

A sheriff's deputy will personally deliver the papers to your spouse. The deputy will fill out a form to verify that the papers were delivered (including the date and time they were delivered), and will file a copy of that form with the court clerk.

OTHER NOTICES

Once your spouse has been served with the petition, you may simply mail him or her copies of any papers you file later. All you need to do is sign a statement (called a *Certificate of Service*) that you mailed copies to your spouse. Some of the forms in this book will have a certificate of service for you to complete. If any form you file does not contain one, you will need to complete the CERTIFICATE OF SERVICE (Form 24), in appendix B of this book. To complete Form 24:

1. Complete the top portion according to the instructions in the first section of this chapter.

2. Type in the name or title of the papers being sent on the first line of the main paragraph.

3. Type in your spouse's name (or your spouse's attorney's name if he or she has an attorney) on the second line in that paragraph.

4. Indicate how the papers are being sent (mailed or hand delivered) by crossing out whichever does not apply.

5. Type in the date the papers are being sent. Be sure to deliver or mail them when you say.

6. Sign your name on the line marked "Name." This form is to be filed with the court clerk as your proof that you sent a copy to your spouse or your spouse's attorney.

When a hearing date is obtained on preliminary matters or temporary orders, you will need to notify your spouse of when the hearing will be. This is done generally by sending a letter to your spouse by personal delivery or certified mail. NOTICE OF HEARING FOR TEMPORARY ORDERS (Form 23) may be used when temporary alimony or temporary child support is requested from the court. To complete Form 23 you need to type in your spouse's name, the address of the court, and the date and time of the hearing on the appropriate lines in the main paragraph. The judge will sign the form, and a copy is sent to your spouse. A general NOTICE OF HEARING form is included as Form 29 and can be changed to fit the particular circumstances, such as whether it is a hearing on a motion, a final hearing, etc.

SETTING A COURT HEARING

When you file your petition, the clerk will generally assign a hearing date that is sixty days from the date of filing. If there are any preliminary matters that require a hearing, the judge's clerk will assign a hearing date.

When you get a hearing date, be sure to ask the clerk where the hearing will be held. You will need the street address of the courthouse, as well as the room number, floor or other location within the building.

Courtroom Manners

There are certain rules of procedure that are used in court. These are really the rules of good conduct, or good manners, and are designed to keep things orderly. Many of the rules are written down, although some are unwritten customs that have just developed over many years. They aren't difficult, and most of them do make sense. Following these suggestions will make the judge respect you for your maturity and professional manner, and possibly even make him forget for a moment that you are not a lawyer. It will also increase the likelihood that you will get the things you request.

Show respect for the judge. This basically means don't do anything to make the judge angry at you, such as arguing with him. Be polite, and call the judge "Your Honor" when you speak to him, such as "Yes, Your Honor," or "Your Honor, I brought proof of my income." Although many, many lawyers address judges as "Judge," this is not proper. Many of the following rules also relate to showing respect for the court. This also means wearing appropriate clothing, such as a coat and tie for men and a dress for women. This especially means no T-shirts, blue jeans, shorts, or "revealing" clothing.

Whenever the judge talks, you listen. Even if the judge interrupts you, stop talking immediately and listen.

Only one person can talk at a time. Each person is allotted his or her own time to talk in court. The judge can only listen to one person at a time, so don't interrupt your spouse when it's his or her turn. And as difficult as it may be, stop talking if your spouse interrupts you. (Let the judge tell your spouse to keep quiet and let you have your say.)

Talk to the judge, not to your spouse. Many people get in front of a judge and begin arguing with each other. They actually turn away from the judge, face each other, and begin arguing as if they are in the room alone. This generally has several negative results: The judge can't understand what either one is saying since they both start talking at once, they both look like fools for losing control, and the judge gets angry with both of them. So whenever you speak in a courtroom, look only at the judge. Try to pretend that your spouse isn't there. Remember, you are there to convince the judge that you should have certain things. You don't need to convince your spouse.

Talk only when it's your turn. The usual procedure is for you to present your case first. When you are done saying all you came to say, your spouse will have a chance to say whatever he or she came to say. Let your spouse have his or her say. When he or she is finished you will get another chance to respond to what has been said.

Stick to the subject. Many people can't resist the temptation to get off the track and start telling the judge all the problems with their marriage over the past twenty years. This just wastes time and aggravates the judge. So stick to the subject and answer the judge's questions simply and to the point.

Keep calm. Judges like things to go smoothly in their courtrooms. They don't like shouting, name calling, crying, or other displays of emotion. Generally, judges don't like family law cases because they get too emotionally charged. Give your judge a pleasant surprise by keeping calm and focusing on the issues.

Show respect for your spouse. Even if you don't respect your spouse, act like you do. All you have to do is refer to your spouse as "Mr. Smith" or "Ms. Smith" (using his or her correct name, of course).

NEGOTIATING SETTLEMENTS

It is beyond the scope and ability of this book to fully present a course in negotiation techniques. However, a few basic rules may be of some help.

Ask for more than you want. This always gives you some room to compromise by giving up a few things, and end up with close to what you really want. With property division, this means you will review your PROPERTY INVENTORY (Form l), and decide which items you really want, would like to have, and don't care much about. Also try to figure out which items your spouse really wants, would like to have, and doesn't care much about. At the beginning you will say that you want certain things. Your list will include: (a) Everything you really want, (b) almost everything you'd like to have, (c) some of the things you don't care about, and (d) some of the things you think your spouse really wants or would like to have. Once you find out what is on your spouse's list, you begin trading items. Generally you try to give your spouse things that he or she really wants and that you don't care about, in return for your spouse giving you the items you really care about and would like to have.

Generally, child custody tends to be something that cannot be negotiated. It is more often used as a threat by one of the parties in order to get something else, such as more of the property, or lower child support. If the real issue is one of these other matters, don't be concerned by a threat of a custody fight. In these cases the other party probably doesn't really want custody, and won't fight for it. If the real issue is custody, you won't be able to negotiate for it and will end up letting the judge decide anyway.

If you will be receiving child support you should first work out what you think the judge will order based upon the child support guidelines discussed in chapter 5. Then you should ask for more, and negotiate down to what the guidelines call for. If your spouse won't settle for something very close to the guidelines, give up trying to work it out and let the judge decide.

Let your spouse start the bidding. The first person to mention a dollar figure loses. Whether it's a child support figure or the value of a piece of property, try to get your spouse to name the amount he or she thinks it should be first. If your spouse starts with a figure almost what you had in mind, it will be much easier to get to your figure. If your spouse begins with a figure far from yours, you know how far in the other direction to begin your bid.

Give your spouse time to think and worry. Your spouse is probably just as afraid as you about the possibility of losing to the judge's decision, and would like to settle. Don't be afraid to state your "final offer," then walk away. Give your spouse a day or two to think it over. Maybe he or she will call back and make a better offer. And if not, you can always "reconsider" and make a different offer in a few days, but don't be too willing to do this or your spouse may think you will give in even more.

Know your bottom line. Before you begin negotiating you should try to set a point which you will not go beyond. If you have decided that there are four items of property that you absolutely must have, and your spouse is only willing to agree to let you have three, it's time to end the bargaining session and go home.

Remember what you've learned. By the time you've read this far you should be aware of two things:

1. The judge will roughly divide your property equally.

2. The judge will probably come close to the child support guidelines.

This awareness should give you an approximate idea of how things will turn out if the judge is asked to decide these issues, which should help you to set your bottom line on them.

Uncontested Divorce Procedure 7

This chapter will provide a general overview of the standard divorce procedure. The following chapters will discuss some of these procedures in more detail.

Contested or Uncontested Divorce

Most lawyers have had the following experience: A new client comes in, saying she wants to file for divorce. She has discussed it with her husband, and it will be a "simple, uncontested" divorce. Once the papers are filed the husband and wife begin arguing over a few items of property. The lawyer then spends a lot of time negotiating with the husband. After much arguing, an agreement is finally reached. The case will proceed in the court as "uncontested," but only after a lot of "contesting" out of court.

For purposes of this book, a *contested* case is where you and your spouse will be doing your arguing in court, and will be leaving the decision to the judge. An *uncontested* case is where you will do your arguing and deciding before court, and the judge will only be approving your decision.

You probably won't know if you are going to have a contested case until you try the uncontested route and fail. Therefore, the following sections are presented mostly to assist you in attempting the uncontested case. Chapter 8 specifically discusses the contested case.

There are actually two ways that a case can be considered "uncontested." One is where you and your spouse reach an agreement on every issue in the divorce. To be in this situation you must be in agreement on the following points:

1. How your property is to be divided.

2. How your debts are to be divided.

3. Which of you will have custody of the children.

4. How much child support is to be paid by the person not having custody.

The other type of uncontested case is where your spouse simply doesn't respond to the petition. If you have your spouse served by the sheriff (as described in chapter 6), and he or she does not respond, you will need to file certain forms.

To begin your divorce case, you should file with the court clerk an ORIGINAL PETITION FOR DIVORCE. Various forms of the petition are included for your use depending on what particular circumstances apply. This will be discussed in greater detail later in this chapter.

It may be necessary to file other forms either with your petition or prior to the final hearing. The following forms will be prepared in advance but will not be filed until the final hearing:

1. DECREE OF DIVORCE

2. STATEMENT OF EVIDENCE

3. ORDER WITHHOLDING FROM EARNINGS FOR CHILD SUPPORT (if you have children)

The following sections give instructions for when you need each form, and how to complete it.

PETITION FOR DIVORCE

An Original Petition for Divorce must be completed in all cases. The petition is simply the paper you file with the court to begin your case and to ask the judge to give you a divorce. The particular form to be used will depend upon your particular circumstances. For instance, Forms 4, 5, 6, or 7 will be used if there are no minor children involved. The difference between these forms deals with the way by which you notify your spouse and whether you request temporary alimony.

Form 4 will be used if you and your spouse are in agreement about everything. If Form 4 is used you must also file a WAIVER OF CITATION (Form 10).

Form 5 will be used if you request that your spouse be notified of the divorce case by personal service (discussed earlier in chapter 6).

Form 6 will be used if you cannot locate your spouse. This is discussed in greater detail in chapter 10.

Form 7 will be used if you are asking the court to order your spouse to pay you temporary alimony until the divorce becomes final. Paragraph II of Form 7 provides for personal service of the petition. If your spouse cannot be located this form must be adapted (using the language contained in paragraph II of Form 6) and you must use the procedure discussed in chapter 10.

Form 8 will be used if you and your spouse have minor children and you are asking the court to order your spouse to pay temporary child support until the divorce becomes final. Paragraph II of Form 8 provides for personal service of the petition. If your spouse cannot be located, Form 9 should be used following the procedure outlined in chapter 10.

When there are minor children involved but you do not request that the judge order temporary child support, Form 8 should be changed to delete the request for temporary orders. This generally occurs when you

65

and your spouse have made arrangements between yourselves regarding the payment of child support.

No matter which form you use, if you are requesting that your spouse pay alimony (called *maintenance* in Texas) after the DECREE OF DIVORCE is entered by the court, you must adapt your PETITION FOR DIVORCE to include a request for maintenance. The added language is included on page 74. Maintenance after a DECREE OF DIVORCE is only possible in a few narrow situations, and you will notice that there are alternative paragraphs that can be used for each of these situations. Choose the paragraph that best suits your situation. Page 74 also has the wording that must be added to you DECREE OF DIVORCE if the judge grants your request for maintenance.

To complete any of the PETITION FOR DIVORCE forms you must:

1. Complete the top portion of the form according to the instructions in chapter 6.

2. Fill in your name, social security number, age and county of residence as the "Petitioner" in the spaces in the first paragraph.

3. Fill in your spouse's name, social security number, age and county of residence (if known) as "Respondent" in the appropriate spaces in the same paragraph.

4. In paragraph I, fill in the county of your residence for the past six months.

5. Paragraph II, of the form you choose designates how notice is to be given to your spouse.

6. In paragraph III, indicate the date and place of your marriage and the date on which you and your spouse stopped living together. If you and your spouse have not separated, cross out the words in the brackets.

7. In paragraph IV, state the names, birthdate, residence and social security number of each minor child, if there are any (forms 8 and 9 only).

8. If you are requesting that your name be changed back to what it was prior to your marriage, indicate your full name as you wish it to be after your divorce.

9. In paragraph VII you must state whether or not a protective order has been entered against one of the parties to the divorce. If a protective order has been entered, you must supply the court with a copy of the order.

10. On the last page, sign your name under "Respectfully submitted" and type your name, address, and phone number on the lines provided.

11. If you are requesting that temporary support be paid until the divorce becomes final, you will need to provide the court with convincing evidence of your spouse's income. This can often be obtained from the documents you collected to complete the PROPERTY INVENTORY (Form 1). If you have no convincing evidence of income, the best procedure is to obtain a subpoena duces tecum for employment records. Attach Form 27 from appendix B to the subpoena. Form 27 is an exhibit which identifies the records you need. You will request that a subpoena be issued when you file the PETITION FOR DIVORCE. This will be discussed in greater detail in chapter 8.

12. If you are requesting that temporary support be paid, you should include a NOTICE OF HEARING (Form 23) with your petition. This will be completed by the court clerk when you file your PETITION FOR DIVORCE.

13. If you are asking that the court order maintenance to be paid after the divorce becomes final, you will need to request this and provide the court with convincing evidence that you cannot support yourself and need the assistance from your spouse.

14. You must include a statement of alternative dispute resolution and sign the statement at the end. This statement is included as part of the PETITION FOR DIVORCE.

Your PETITION FOR DIVORCE is now ready for filing. Take it to the courthouse and follow the procedure for filing as explained in chapter 6.

WAIVER OF CITATION

If your spouse agrees to everything that you are asking the court to do, your spouse should file a WAIVER OF CITATION (Form 10) with the court. To complete the WAIVER OF CITATION (Form 10) you must:

1. Complete the top portion of the form according to the instructions in chapter 6.

2. Type in your spouse's name in the blank space in the first paragraph.

3. Type in your spouse's name and address in the second paragraph.

4. Have your spouse sign the line directly under "Respectfully submitted" in the presence of a notary public. Have the notary public complete the rest of the form.

ANSWER

If you and your spouse agree on everything and your spouse files a WAIVER OF CITATION, you do not need to file a RESPONDENT'S ORIGINAL ANSWER (Form 12). However, if your spouse does not agree with everything, an ANSWER should be filed with the court.

To complete the RESPONDENT'S ORIGINAL ANSWER (Form 12) you must:

1. Complete the top portion of the form according to the instructions in chapter 6.

2. Type in your spouse's name in the blank space in the first paragraph.

3. Type in your spouse's name, address, and phone number where indicated at the bottom of the form.

4. Have your spouse sign the line directly under the words "Respectfully submitted."

5. Have your spouse sign the line directly under the statement on the alternative dispute resolution.

MARITAL SETTLEMENT AGREEMENT

If you and your spouse agree on the division of your assets, you may prepare a Marital Settlement Agreement (Form 25). This spells out how your property and debts will be divided.

Complete the MARITAL SETTLEMENT AGREEMENT (Form 25) as follows:

1. Complete the top portion according to the instructions in Chapter 6.

2. Type in your name, your spouse's name and your social security numbers, ages, and counties of residence in the appropriate spaces in the first (unnumbered) paragraph.

3. In paragraph I, type in the county in which you have resided for the ninety days preceding the date when you filed the petition.

4. Type in the date of your marriage, the city and state where you were married, and the date of your separation in paragraph II.

If you and your spouse have not separated, cross out the words in the brackets.

5. In paragraph V, list the items of property to be kept by the person designated as the "Petitioner" (this is the person whose name appears first in the case style heading, which will probably be you). Be as specific as possible in describing the items. However, you do not need to include every little item in the house, but you should include all major items.

6. In paragraph VI, list the items the "Respondent" (your spouse) will keep.

7. In paragraph VII, list the debts the petitioner will pay.

8. In paragraph VIII, list the debts the respondent will pay.

9. After the paragraph beginning with the word "WHEREFORE," type in you and your spouse's names, addresses, and telephone numbers where indicated. DO NOT SIGN YOUR NAMES YET!

10. Take this form to a notary public, and sign your names before the notary. The notary public will complete the rest of the form. There are two notary spaces on the last page of this form, one for you and one for your spouse. This is so both you and your spouse don't need to go to the notary at the same time (or to the same notary).

This form should be filed with the court prior to the day you are scheduled to have a hearing on your petition.

TEMPORARY SUPPORT

If temporary support has been requested, the court will set a hearing on your request. Your spouse should be sent a NOTICE OF HEARING FOR TEMPORARY ORDERS (Form 23). See the section on NOTIFYING YOUR

SPOUSE in chapter 6 for more information about Form 23. You should have ready at the hearing a TEMPORARY ORDERS form (Form 14 or Form 15). Use Form 14 if there are no children involved. Use Form 15 if you are also seeking temporary child support. To complete either Form 14 or Form 15 you must:

1. Complete the top portion according to the instructions in chapter 6.

2. Fill in your name and your spouse's name where appropriate.

3. Fill in the name of the parent who will have custody of the children.

Leave blank the amount and timing of the support payments, as the judge will decide these questions at the hearing. You should attach the STANDARD POSSESSION ORDER (Form 22) to the TEMPORARY ORDERS form in order to govern visitation rights. After the TEMPORARY ORDERS form is signed, you will need to send a copy to your spouse.

DECREE OF DIVORCE

A DECREE OF DIVORCE (Form 16, 17, and 18) will be completed in all cases. You should complete as much of the form as possible before the hearing. The form is designed so that you can complete it at the hearing according to what the judge decides on each issue. You can complete ahead of time any items that you and your spouse have agreed upon. Give your spouse a copy of the DECREE OF DIVORCE before the hearing, so that he or she can tell the judge that he or she is aware of what it says, and agrees.

If your spouse has waived citation, you may go to the courthouse on the day of your hearing and *prove-up* your petition. Generally, a prove-up consists of testimony in the form of restating the principal allegations of your petition. Take your time and recite to the judge the most important points of the petition and what it is that you are asking the court to do—grant you a divorce, divide your property, and change your name (if requested).

If maintenance (alimony) was awarded, be sure to follow the instructions on page 74, and add the appropriate provisions from page 74 to the DECREE OF DIVORCE.

If your spouse has not responded by filing a waiver or an answer, you may bring to the hearing a DEFAULT CERTIFICATE (Form 26) if your spouse was served in person, or a STATEMENT OF EVIDENCE (Forms 20 or 21) if your spouse was served by publication. If your spouse was served by publication and children are involved, the court will have appointed an attorney ad litem to represent the interests of the children. This attorney ad litem generally will be present at the prove-up and will also sign the STATEMENT OF EVIDENCE. If child support is ordered by the court, bring with you an ORDER WITHHOLDING FROM EARNINGS FOR CHILD SUPPORT (Form 19).

After the DECREE OF DIVORCE, STATEMENT OF EVIDENCE, and ORDER WITHHOLDING FROM EARNINGS FOR CHILD SUPPORT are signed by the judge, fill in any blanks left by the judge for you to complete. Have several copies conformed by the court clerk. *Conformed* copies are ones which have the judge's stamped signature on it. The clerk will keep the original and you should get at least two conformed copies. Mail a conformed copy of the DECREE OF DIVORCE to your spouse by registered mail. By certified mail send a copy of the ORDER WITHHOLDING EARNINGS FOR CHILD SUPPORT to your spouse's employer. The Child Support Office may have additional forms that you may need to complete and file with it. You should be sure to check with this office as to what additional forms you need to complete to make certain that the child support order is correctly implemented.

ORDER WITHHOLDING FROM EARNINGS FOR CHILD SUPPORT

An ORDER WITHHOLDING FROM EARNINGS FOR CHILD SUPPORT (Form 19) must be completed whenever child support is ordered. This is an order to the employer of the person required to make the payment, requiring the employer to deduct the payment from the person's paycheck and send it to the Child Support Office. This form can be completed prior to the final hearing and presented to the judge for signature.

To complete the ORDER WITHHOLDING FROM EARNINGS FOR CHILD SUPPORT (Form 19):

1. Complete the top portion of the form according to the instructions in chapter 6.

2. Type in the name, address, social security number and driver's license number of the person who must pay support (you or your spouse) on the lines for "Obligor."

3. Type in the name, address, social security number and driver's license number of the person who will receive support (you or your spouse) on the lines for "Obligee."

4. Type in the name, address, social security number, driver's license number, birthdate, and birthplace of each child who will receive support on the appropriate lines.

5. Type in the appropriate amount of earnings to be withheld by using lines (1), (2), (3), or (4) on the second page of this form.

6. Type in the name and address of the agency to which the support payments must be mailed. Also include the child support account number that has been assigned. The information necessary to complete this section can be obtained from the court clerk.

7. Leave this form with the judge's clerk, who will process it or direct you as to where you should take it.

SPECIAL PROVISIONS FOR MAINTENANCE (ALIMONY)

PETITION FOR DIVORCE: If you are asking that your spouse pay maintenance after the Decree of Divorce is entered by the court, you must adapt your PETITION FOR DIVORCE form, following these instructions:

1. Add the following paragraph: "Petitioner requests the Court to order Respondent to pay maintenance to Petitoner for a reasonable period after the divorce is granted."

2. Add one (and only one)of the following paragraphs:

   a. "Respondent was convicted of (received deferred adjudication for) an offense that also constitutes an act of family violence under Section 71.01, Family Code, and the offense occurred within two years before the date on which this suit was filed/during the pendency of this suit."

   b. "Petitioner would show the Court that the parties have been married more than 10 years, and that Petitioner is unable to support himself/herself due to an incapacitating physical or mental disability. Petitioner requests the Court to order Respondent to pay maintenance to Petitioner for an indefinite period of time for as long as the disability continues."

   c. "Petitioner would show the Court that the parties have been married more than 10 years, and that Petitioner lacks sufficient property, including property to be distributed to Petitioner under the Texas Family Code, to provide for Petitioner's minimum reasonable needs, and"

   If you added paragraph "c," then you will need to add one or both of the following paragraphs:

   i. "Petitioner is the custodian of a child who requires substantial care and personal supervision because a physical or mental diability makes it necessary, taking into consideration the needs of the child, that Petitioner not be employed outside the home."

   ii. "Petitioner clearly lacks earning ability in the labor market adequate to provide support for Petitioner's minimum reasonable needs."

DECREE OF DIVORCE: If maintenance was ordered by the judge, you must adapt your DECREE OF DIVORCE form , following these instructions (for words or phrases in brackets "{ }," selected one of the choices):

1. Add one or both of the following paragraphs:

   a. "The Court finds that Respondent {was convicted of} {received deferred adjudication for} an offense that also constitutes an act of family violence under Section 71.01, Family Code, and the offense occurred {within two years before the date on which this suit was filed} {during the pendency of this suit}."

   b. "The Court finds that the parties have been married more than 10 years, and that Petitioner lacks sufficient property, including property to be distributed to Petitioner under the Texas Family Code, to provide for Petitioner's minimum reasonable needs, and"

   If you added paragraph "b," then you will also need to add one or more of the following paragraphs:

   i. "The Court finds that Petitioner is unable to support {himself} {herself} through appropriate employment due to an incapacitating physical or mental disability."

   ii. "The Court finds that Petitioner is the custodian of a child who requires substantial care and personal supervision because a physical or mental disability makes it necessary, taking into consideration the needs of the child, that Petitioner not be employed outside the home."

   iii. "The Court finds that Petitioner clearly lacks earning ability in the labor market adequate to provide support for Petitioner's minimum reasonable needs.

2. Add the following paragraph (filling in the amounts and dates): "IT IS ORDERED AND DECREED that RESPONDENT is obligated to pay and shall pay to PETITIONER maintenance of $_____ per month, in two equal payments of $_____ each, with the first payment of $_____ being due and payable on the ___ day of _____, ____, and like payments being due and payable on the ____ and ____ days of each month thereafter until the date of the earliest occurrence of one of the following events:
   1. Death of the Petitioner.
   2. _____, _____.
   3. Petitioner is cohabiting with another person in a permanent place of abode on a continuing, conjugal basis.
   4. Further order of this Court regarding maintenance."

Contested Divorce Procedure 8

Procedure Differences from Uncontested Divorce

This book cannot turn you into a trial lawyer. It can be very risky to try to handle a contested case yourself, although it has been done. There are several differences between a contested and an uncontested case. First, in an uncontested case the judge will usually go along with whatever you and your spouse have worked out. In a contested case you need to prove that you are entitled to what you are asking for. This means you will need a longer time for the hearing, you will need to present papers as evidence, and you may need to have witnesses testify for you.

Second, you may have to do some extra work to get the evidence you need, such as sending out subpoenas (which are discussed in the next section of this chapter), or even hiring a private investigator.

Also, you will need to pay extra attention to assure that your spouse is properly notified of any court hearings, and that he or she is sent copies of any papers you file with the court clerk.

When it becomes apparent that you have a contested divorce, it is probably time to consider hiring an attorney, especially if the issue of child custody is involved. If you are truly ready to go to war over custody, it is an extremely important matter to you, and you may want to get professional assistance. You can predict a contested case when your spouse is seriously threatening to fight you every inch of the way, or when he or she hires an attorney.

On the other hand, you shouldn't assume that you need an attorney just because your spouse has hired one. Sometimes it will be easier to deal with the attorney than with your spouse. The attorney is not as emotionally involved and may see your settlement proposal as reasonable. So discuss things with your spouse's attorney first and see if things can be worked out. You can always hire your own lawyer if your spouse's isn't reasonable. Just be very cautious about signing any papers until you are certain you understand what they mean. You may want to have an attorney review any papers prepared by your spouse's lawyer before you sign them.

Aside from deciding if you want a lawyer, there are two main procedure differences between the uncontested and the contested divorce. First, you will need to be more prepared for the hearing. Second, you will not prepare the DECREE OF DIVORCE until after the hearing with the judge. This is because you won't know what to put in the DECREE OF DIVORCE until the judge decides the various matters in dispute.

COLLECTING INFORMATION

If there is a dispute over property, the judge may require an *Inventory and Appraisement* form from you, and also one from your spouse. (This form can be obtained from the judge, clerk, or law library.) You may also be able to use a signed copy of Form 1 and Form 2 instead. If your spouse has indicated that he or she will not cooperate at all, and will not provide an Inventory and Appraisement, you may have to try to get the information yourself. You can go to the hearing and tell the judge that your spouse won't cooperate, but the judge may just issue an order requiring your spouse to provide information (or be held in contempt of court) and continue the hearing to another date. It may help to speed things up if you are able to get the information yourself and have it available at the hearing. This will require you to get subpoenas issued.

Before you send a subpoena to your spouse's employer, bank, or accountant, you need to let your spouse know what you are about to do. The thought that you are about to get these other people involved in your divorce may be enough to get your spouse to cooperate. If your spouse calls and says "I'll give you the information," give him or her a few days to follow through. Ask when you can expect to receive the Inventory and Appraisement, and offer to send your spouse another blank copy if he or she needs one. If your spouse sends a completed Inventory and Appraisement as promised, don't send the subpoena. If your spouse doesn't follow through, go ahead with the subpoena. You can send out subpoenas to as many people or organizations as you need, but you'll need to use the following procedure for each subpoena.

You will request the clerk to give you a form for a subpoena for employment records. This form will eventually be sent to whomever you want to get information from. If you were able to do a good job making copies of important papers while preparing to file for divorce, you should have the information you need to figure out where you need to send subpoenas. Your spouse's income information can be obtained from his or her employer. Stock and bond information can be obtained from his or her stock broker, bank account balances from the bank, auto loan balances from the lender, etc. You can have subpoenas issued to any or all of these places, but don't overdo it. Concentrate on income information (especially if you are asking for child support or expect to pay child support) and information on the major property items. And, it may not be necessary to send out subpoenas if you already have recent copies of the papers relating to these items. You can always show the judge the copies of your spouse's paystubs, W-2 tax statements, or other papers at the hearing. Form 27 is an exhibit that you may wish to attach to the subpoena. Form 28 can be provided to the person you seek records from. If completed, and signed before a notary, it allows them to verify the records as being authentic, and avoid having to appear for a deposition or hearing.

Next, have the sheriff personally serve the subpoena to the person or place named in the subpoena. The sheriff will need at least one extra copy of the subpoena and a check for the service fee. The employer, bank, etc., should send you the requested information. If the employer calls you and says you must pay for copies, ask him how much they will cost and send a check or money order (if the amount isn't too high and you don't already have some fairly recent income information). If the employer doesn't provide the information, you can try sending a letter to the employer saying: "unless you provide the information requested in the subpoena in seven days, a motion for contempt will be filed with the circuit court." This may scare the employer into sending you the information. The sheriff will have also filed an affidavit verifying when the subpoena was served. There are more procedures you could go through to force the employer to give the information, but it probably isn't worth the hassle and you'd probably need an attorney to help you with it. At the final hearing you can tell the judge that your spouse refused to provide income information, and that the subpoena was not honored by the employer. The judge may do something to help you out, or he may advise you to see a lawyer.

There is also a procedure in which you send written questions to your spouse, that he or she must answer in writing and under oath. These written questions are called *interrogatories*. If your spouse didn't file an Inventory and Appraisement, he or she probably won't answer the interrogatories either, which would leave you no better off. However, if you would like to try this, you may be able to locate the forms you would need at the clerk's office or law library.

Once you collect the information needed, you can prepare for the hearing.

PROPERTY AND DEBTS

Generally, the judge will look at your property and debts, and will try to divide them "fairly." This does not mean they will necessarily be divided fifty-fifty. What you want to do is offer the judge a reasonable solution that looks "fair."

It's time to review the PROPERTY INVENTORY (Form 1) and the DEBT INVENTORY (Form 2) you prepared earlier. For each item or property note which of the following categories it fits into (it may fit into more than one):

1. You really want.

2. You'd like to have.

3. You don't care either way.

4. Your spouse really wants.

5. Your spouse would like to have.

6. Your spouse doesn't care either way.

Now start a list of what each of you should end up with, using the categories listed above. You will eventually end up with a list of things you can probably get with little difficulty (you really want and your spouse doesn't care), those which you'll fight over (you both really want), and those which need to be divided but can probably be easily divided equally (you both don't really care).

At the hearing the judge will probably try to get you to work out your disagreements, but he won't put up with arguing for very long. In the end he will arbitrarily divide the items you can't agree upon, or may order you to sell those items and divide the money you get equally.

On the few items that are really important to you it may be necessary for you to try to prove why you should get them. It will help if you can convince the judge of one or more of the following:

1. You paid for the item out of your own earnings or funds.

2. You are the one who primarily uses that item.

3. You use the item in your employment, business, or hobby.

4. You are willing to give up something else you really want in exchange for that item. (Of course you will try to give up something from your "don't care" or your "like to have" list.)

5. The item is needed for your children (assuming you will have custody).

The best thing you can do is make up a list of how you think the property should be divided. Make it a reasonably fair and equal list, regardless of how angry you are at your spouse. Even if the judge changes some of it to appear fair to your spouse, you will most likely get more of what you want than if you don't offer a suggestion. (No, this is not an exception to the negotiating rule of letting your spouse make the first offer, because at this point you are no longer just negotiating with your spouse. You are now negotiating with the judge. At this point you are trying to impress the judge with your fairness; not trying to convince your spouse.)

Special problems arise if a claim of separate property becomes an issue. This may be in terms of your spouse trying to get your separate property, or in terms of you trying to get property you feel your spouse is wrongly claiming to be separate. Basically, separate property is property either of you had before you were married, and kept separate.

It is also a good idea to have any papers which prove that the property you claim to be separate property is actually separate property. These would be papers showing that:

☛ You bought the item before you were married (such as dated sales receipts).

☛ You were given or inherited the item as your own property (such as certified copies of wills and probate court papers).

☛ You got the property by exchanging it for property you had before you got married, or for property you received as a gift or through an inheritance (such as a statement from the person you made the exchange with, or some kind of receipt showing what was exchanged).

If you want to get at assets your spouse is claiming are separate assets, you will need to collect the following types of evidence:

☛ Papers showing that you helped pay for the asset (such as a check that you wrote or bank statements showing that your money went into the same account that was used to make payments on the asset). For example, suppose your spouse purchased a house before you got married. During your marriage you made some of the mortgage payments with your own checking account (you will have cancelled checks, hopefully with the mortgage account number on them, to prove this). At other times, you deposited some of your paychecks into your spouse's checking account, and your spouse wrote checks from that account to pay the mortgage (again, there should be some bank records and cancelled checks that show that this was done). Since you contributed to the purchase of the house, you can claim some of the value of the house as a marital asset.

☛ Papers showing that you paid for repairs of the asset. If you paid for repairs on the home, or a car your spouse had before you were married, you can claim part of the value.

☛ Papers showing the asset was improved, or increased in value during your marriage. Example 1: Your spouse owned the house before you were married. During your marriage you and your spouse added a family room to the house. This will enable you to make a claim for some of the value of the house. Example 2: Your spouse owned the house before you were married. The day before you got married, the house was worth

$85,000. Now the house is appraised at $115,000. You can claim part of the $30,000 of increased value.

During the hearing the judge will announce who gets which items. Make a list of this as the judge tells you. Then, complete the DECREE OF DIVORCE according to what the judge says. Once you have completed the DECREE OF DIVORCE, the judge will sign the judgment and return a copy to you. You should send a copy to your spouse.

CHILD CUSTODY AND VISITATION

Generally, if you are the wife, the odds start out in favor of you getting custody. But don't depend upon the odds. Start out by reviewing the guidelines the judge will use to decide the custody question. These can be found in chapter 5. For each item listed in that section, write down an explanation of how that item applies to you. This will be your argument when you have your hearing with the judge.

Many custody battles revolve around the moral fitness of one or both of the parents. If you become involved in this type of a custody fight, you should consult a lawyer. Charges of moral unfitness (such as illegal drug use, child abuse, immoral sexual conduct) can require long court hearings involving the testimony of many witnesses, as well as possibly the employment of private investigators. For such a hearing you will require the help of an attorney who knows the law, knows what questions to ask witnesses, and understands the rules of evidence.

However, if the only question is whether you or your spouse has been the main caretaker of the child, you can always have friends, neighbors, and relatives come into the hearing (if they are willing to help you out) to testify on your behalf. It may not be necessary for you to have an attorney. But, if you need to subpoena unwilling witnesses to testify, you should have an attorney.

The judge's decision regarding custody will have to be put into the DECREE OF DIVORCE. Read chapter 7 for instructions on preparing the DECREE OF DIVORCE.

CHILD SUPPORT

In Texas, as in most states, the question of child support is mostly a matter of a mathematical calculation. Getting a fair child support amount depends upon the accuracy of the income information presented to the judge. If you feel fairly sure that the information your spouse presents is accurate, or that you have obtained accurate information about his or her income, there isn't much to argue about. The judge will simply take the income information provided, use the formula to calculate the amount to be paid, and order that amount to be paid.

In most cases, there won't be much room to argue about the amount of child support, so there usually isn't a need to get an attorney. If you claim your spouse has not provided accurate income information, it will be up to you to prove this to the judge by showing the income information you have obtained from your spouse's employer or other source of income.

The only areas open for argument are whatever special needs are claimed by the party asking for child support. Once again, it will be necessary for that party to provide proof of the cost of these special needs by producing billing statements, receipts, or other papers to show the amount of these needs.

The judge's decision regarding child support will have to be put into the DECREE OF DIVORCE. Be sure to read chapter 7 for instructions on preparing the DECREE OF DIVORCE.

THE COURT HEARING 9

PREPARATION

SETTING A
HEARING DATE

The first step in preparing for the final hearing is to get a hearing date set.
See chapter 6 for instructions on setting a hearing date.

NOTIFYING
YOUR SPOUSE

Now that you've got a hearing date set with the judge, you'll need to
notify your spouse of when the hearing will be. Even if you can easily call
your spouse on the phone and notify him or her of the hearing, it is also
a good idea to send a formal notice of the hearing by regular or certified
mail.

WHAT
PAPERS TO
BRING

Bring your copies (if available) of the following papers to the hearing:

☞ Your ORIGINAL PETITION FOR DIVORCE.

☞ Any papers you may have showing that your spouse was properly notified of the divorce (although the sheriff's affidavit of
serving papers will be in the court file, and you may not have a
copy).

☞ Any papers you may have to support that property you are
claiming can be awarded to you. This should include copies of
your most recent paystub, Federal income tax return, and W-2
forms.

☞ Any paper's showing your spouse's income or property.

☞ Your MARITAL SETTLEMENT AGREEMENT, if you have one that hasn't yet been filed with the court.

☞ Your proposed DECREE OF DIVORCE.

THE HEARING

Your hearing will probably not take place in a large courtroom like you see on TV or in the movies. It will most likely be in what looks more like a conference room. Generally, the judge will be at the head of a table, with you and your spouse on either side.

The judge may start the hearing by summarizing what you are there for, then ask you and your spouse if you have any additional evidence to present, and then ask each of you any questions he or she may have. The judge will review the papers you filed with the clerk and will probably ask you whether you understand and agree with what is in the papers. The judge will also ask you to explain why you're getting divorced. (Example 1: "We just don't have any interests in common anymore, and have drifted apart." Example 2: "My husband has had several affairs.")

If you have any information that is different and more current than what is in the Inventory and Appraisement forms that may have been filed with the court, you should mention to the judge that you have more current information. You will then give a copy of whatever papers you have to show the changed situation (such as current paystub showing an increase in pay or a current bank statement showing a new balance).

If there are any items that you and your spouse have not yet agreed upon, tell the judge what these items are. Refer to chapter 8, relating to the contested divorce, for more information about how to handle these unresolved issues. Be prepared to make a suggestion as to how these matters should be settled, and to explain to the judge why your suggestion is the best solution.

If the judge asks for any information that you haven't brought with you, tell the judge that you don't have it with you but you will be happy to provide him or her with the information by the end of the following day. Just be sure you get the papers to the judge!

At the end of the hearing the judge will tell you if he or she is going to grant you a divorce and accept your settlement agreement. It would be very unusual not to grant the divorce and accept your agreement. You will then tell the judge that you've prepared a proposed DECREE OF DIVORCE, and hand him or her the original. Refer back to chapter 7, regarding how to prepare the DECREE OF DIVORCE form. You should have two extra copies of the DECREE OF DIVORCE with you, one for yourself and one for your spouse. You should also bring two envelopes, one addressed to yourself and one addressed to your spouse, and two stamps. This is in case the judge wants to review the DECREE OF DIVORCE and mail it to you later, instead of signing it at the hearing. If the judge wants you to make any changes in the DECREE OF DIVORCE, make a careful note of exactly what the judge wants (ask the judge to explain it again if you didn't understand the first time), then tell the judge that you will make the correction and deliver the judgment the following day. If the change requested is a small one, you might even be able to write in the change by hand at the hearing.

If child support or alimony is to be paid, you will also need to bring a third copy of the DECREE OF DIVORCE, and an original and four copies of the ORDER WITHHOLDING FROM EARNINGS FOR CHILD SUPPORT (Form 19). The judge will sign the ORDER WITHHOLDING FROM EARNINGS FOR CHILD SUPPORT at the hearing. The four copies are for you, your spouse, the central depository, and the child support enforcement office (which also gets the additional copy of the judgment).

When the hearing is over, thank the judge and leave. The judge will sign the original DECREE OF DIVORCE, and send it to the court clerk's office to be entered in the court's file. Take the copies of the judgment and withholding order to the clerk. The clerk will write in the date and use a stamp with the judge's name on each copy to authenticate them.

If any serious problems develop at the hearing (such as your spouse's attorney starts making a lot of technical objections, or the judge gives you a hard time), just tell the judge you'd like to continue the hearing so you can retain an attorney. Then go get one!

CHILD SUPPORT
AGENCIES

There are two agencies you need to be aware of:

Child Support Office. The CSO is the agency that processes the child support payments. The spouse responsible to pay the support (or his or her employer) will make payments to the CSO. The CSO then cashes that check and issues a check to the spouse entitled to receive support. The CSO keeps the official records of what has and has not been paid.

Child Support Enforcement Division. The Child Support Enforcement Division is responsible for enforcing the payment of child support to custodial parents receiving welfare (Aid to Families with Dependent Children) and others who request their services. If you are to receive support and you would like to use the enforcement services of this office, you will need to contact your local Child Support Enforcement Division. This may not be necessary if your spouse goes on a withholding order immediately, and keeps his or her job. But if some payments are missed, you may call the Child Support Enforcement Division at any time and ask for their assistance.

REMARRRIAGE

If you are planning to take a new spouse after you get divorced, you should be aware that Texas law prohibits you from marrying for thirty-one days after the date of your DECREE OF DIVORCE. There are two exceptions to this thirty-one day waiting period: (1) if you are re-marrying the person you just divorced, and (2) if you obtain a waiver from the judge "for good cause shown" (see section 6.902 on page 103).

WHEN YOU CAN'T FIND YOUR SPOUSE 10

Your spouse has run off, and you have no idea of where he or she might be. So how do you have the sheriff deliver a copy of your petition to your spouse? The answer is, you can't use the sheriff. Instead of personal service you will use a method of giving notice called *service by publication*. This is one of the most complicated procedures in the legal system. You will need to follow the steps listed below very carefully.

THE DILIGENT SEARCH

The court will only permit publication when you can't locate your spouse. This also includes the situation in which the sheriff has tried several times to personally serve your spouse, but it appears that your spouse is hiding to avoid being served. First, you'll have to show that you can't locate your spouse by letting the court know what you've done to try to find him or her. In making this search you should try the following:

- ☛ Check the phone book and directory assistance in the area where you live.

- ☛ Check directory assistance in the area where you last knew your spouse to be.

☞ Ask friends and relatives who might know where your spouse might be.

☞ Check with the post office where he or she last lived to see if there is a forwarding address. (You can ask by mail if it is too far away.)

☞ Check records of the tax collector and property assessor to see if your spouse owns property.

☞ Write to the Department of Motor Vehicles to see if your spouse has any car registrations.

☞ Check with any other sources you know that may lead you to a current address (such as landlords, prior employers, etc.).

If you do come up with a current address, go back to personal service by the sheriff, but if not, continue with this procedure.

PREPARING AND FILING COURT PAPERS

Once you have made your search you need to notify the court. This is done by filing the AFFIDAVIT FOR CITATION BY PUBLICATION (Form 11). All this form does is tell the court what you've done to try to locate your spouse, and ask for permission to publish your notice. (If your spouse lives in another state, and you do have his or her address, you may use this procedure.) To complete the AFFIDAVIT FOR CITATION BY PUBLICATION (Form 11):

1. Complete the top portion of the form according to the instructions in chapter 6.

2. Type your name in the blank in the first two paragraphs.

3. Type in the name of your spouse in the fourth paragraph.

4. Type in the date.

5. Sign your name on the "Signed" line at the end of the form in front of a notary public.

6. Give the form to a notary public to complete.

PUBLISHING

The clerk will arrange for publication. The notice need only be published once. Get a copy of the paper and check to be sure it was printed correctly. If you find an error, notify the newspaper immediately.

SPECIAL CIRCUMSTANCES 11

WHEN YOU CAN'T AFFORD COURT COSTS

Form 13 is an AFFIDAVIT OF INABILITY TO PAY COURT COSTS. This is for use when you can't afford to pay the filing fee and other costs associated with the divorce.

To complete the AFFIDAVIT OF INABILITY TO PAY COURT COSTS (Form 13):

1. Complete the top portion according to the instructions in chapter 6.

2. Type in your name in the first (unnumbered) paragraph.

3. Complete numbered paragraphs 1 through 8 with as much detail as possible.

4. Sign on the line marked "Affiant" in the presence of a notary public.

5. The notary public will then date and sign the form. The form is now ready for filing.

PROTECTING YOURSELF, YOUR CHILDREN, AND YOUR PROPERTY

Some people have two special concerns when preparing to file for a divorce: Fear of physical attack by their spouse, and fear that their spouse will try to take the marital property and hide it. There are additional legal papers you can file if you feel you are in either of these situations.

PROTECTING
YOURSELF

If you fear violence from your spouse, contact the court clerk's office and ask for information and assistance in filing papers to prevent domestic violence. This subject is covered in the Texas Family Code, beginning with section 3.581.

PROTECTING
YOUR PROPERTY

If you genuinely fear that your spouse will try to remove money from bank accounts and try to hide important papers showing what property you own, you may want to take this same action before your spouse can. However, you can make a great deal of trouble for yourself with the judge if you do this to try to get these assets for yourself. So, make a complete list of any property you do take, and be sure to include these items in your Inventory and Appraisment form. You may need to convince the judge that you only took these items temporarily, in order to preserve them until a DECREE OF DIVORCE is entered. Also, do not spend any cash you take from a bank account, or sell or give away any items of property you take. Any cash should be placed in a separate bank account, without your spouse's name on it, and kept separate from any other cash you have. Any papers, such as deeds, car titles, stock or bond certificates, etc., should be placed in a safe deposit box, without your spouse's name on it. The idea is not to take these things for yourself, but to get them in a safe place so your spouse can't hide them and deny they ever existed.

PROTECTING
YOUR
CHILDREN

If you are worried that your spouse may try to kidnap your children, you should make sure that the day care center, babysitter, relative, or whomever you leave the children with at any time, is aware that you are in the process of a divorce and that the children are only to be released to you personally (not to your spouse or to any other relative, friend, etc.). To prevent your spouse from taking the children out of the United States, you can apply for a passport for each child. Once a passport is issued, the government will not issue another. So get their passports and lock them up in a safe deposit box. (This won't prevent them from being taken to Canada or Mexico, where passports are not required, but will prevent them from being taken overseas.)

You can also file a motion to prevent the removal of the children from the state and to deny passport services. Forms for this motion are discussed at the beginning of appendix B, in the section titled WHERE TO FIND ADDITIONAL FORMS.

If your spouse is determined and resourceful, there is no guaranteed way to prevent the things discussed in this chapter from happening. All you can do is put as many obstacles in his or her way as possible, and prepare for him or her to suffer legal consequences for acting improperly.

TEMPORARY SUPPORT AND CUSTODY

If your spouse has left you with the children and the mortgage and monthly bills, and is not helping you out financially, you may want to consider asking the court to order the payment of support for you and the children during the divorce procedure. Of course, if you were the only person bringing in income and have been paying all the bills, don't expect to get any temporary support.

You will need to use one of the petition forms which include a request for temporary support (Forms 7, 8, or 9) and a TEMPORARY ORDERS form (Forms 14 and 15). These are discussed in greater detail in chapter 7.

TAXES

As you are no doubt aware, the United States' income tax code is complicated and ever-changing. For this reason it is impossible to give detailed legal advice with respect to taxes in a book such as this. Any such information could easily be out of date by the time of publication. Therefore, it is strongly recommended that you consult your accountant, lawyer, or whomever prepares your tax return, about the tax consequences of a divorce. A few general concerns are discussed in this chapter, to give you an idea of some of the tax questions that can arise.

TAXES AND PROPERTY

You and your spouse may be exchanging title to property as a result of your divorce. Generally, there will not be any tax to pay as the result of such a transfer. However, whomever gets a piece of property will be responsible to pay any tax that may become due upon sale.

The Internal Revenue Service (I.R.S.) has issued numerous rulings about how property is to be treated in divorce situations. You need to be especially careful if you are transferring any tax shelters, or other complicated financial arrangements.

Be sure to read the following section on alimony, because fancy property settlements are asking for tax problems.

TAXES AND ALIMONY

Alimony can cause the most tax problems of any aspect of divorce. I.R.S. is always making new rulings on whether an agreement is really *alimony*, or is really *property division*. The basic rule is that *alimony* is treated as income to the person receiving it, and as a deduction for the person paying it. Therefore, in order to manipulate the tax consequences, many couples try to show something as part of the property settlement, instead of as alimony; or the reverse. As I.R.S. becomes aware of these "tax games" it issues rulings on how it will view a certain arrangement. If you are simply talking about the regular, periodic payment of cash, I.R.S. will probably not question that it is alimony. But, if you try to call it property settlement you may run into problems. The important thing is to consult a tax expert if you are considering any unusual or creative property settlement or alimony arrangements.

TAXES AND
CHILD SUPPORT

There are simple tax rules regarding child support:

1. Whoever has custody gets to claim the children on his or her tax return (unless both parents file a special I.R.S. form agreeing to a different arrangement each year).

2. The parent receiving child support does not need to report it as income.

3. The parent paying child support cannot deduct it.

If you are sharing physical custody, the parent with whom the child lives for the most time during the year is entitled to claim the child as a dependent.

The I.R.S. form to reverse this must be filed each year. Therefore, if you and your spouse have agreed that you will get to claim the children (even though you don't have custody), you should get your spouse to sign an open-ended form that you can file each year, so that you don't have to worry about it each year. A phone call to the I.R.S. can help you get answers to questions on this point.

PENSION PLANS

Pension plans, or retirement plans, of you and your spouse are marital assets. They may be very valuable assets. If you and your spouse are young, and have not been working very long, you may not have pension plans worth worrying about. Also, if you have both worked, and have similar pensions plans, it may be best just to include a provision in your settlement agreement that "each party shall keep his or her own pension plan." But if you have been married a long time, and one of you worked while the other stayed home to raise the children, the pension plan may be worth a lot of money and may be necessary to see you through retirement. If you and your spouse cannot agree on how to divide a pension plan, you should see an attorney. The valuation of pension plans, and how they are to be divided, is a complicated matter that you should not attempt.

APPENDIX A
TEXAS FAMILY CODE

The following are portions of the *Texas Family Code* relating to various aspects of divorce. These are not all of the provisions relating to divorce, but only some of the more significant ones. Comments that are not part of these laws are in brackets, "[ ]." For more information, refer to the most recent version of the *Texas Family Code*. This can be found at many libraries, and at all law libraries. Remember, the title on these books will be: *Vernon's Texas Codes Annotated.* Look for the volume marked "Family Code."

TITLE 1. THE MARRIAGE RELATIONSHIP

SUBTITLE B. PROPERTY RIGHTS AND LIABILITIES

CHAPTER 3. MARITAL PROPERTY RIGHTS AND LIABILITIES

SUBCHAPTER A. GENERAL RULES FOR SEPARATE AND COMMUNITY PROPERTY

§ 3.001   Separate Property
A spouse's separate property consists of:
  (1) the property owned or claimed by the spouse before marriage;
  (2) the property acquired by the spouse during marriage by gift, devise, or descent; and
  (3) the recovery for personal injuries sustained by the spouse during the marriage, except any recovery for loss of earning capacity during marriage.

§ 3.002   Community Property
Community property consists of the property, other than separate property, acquired by either spouse during marriage.

§ 3.003. Presumption of Community Property

(a) Property possessed by either spouse during or on dissolution of marriage is presumed to be community property.

(b) The degree of proof necessary to establish that property is separate property is clear and convincing evidence.

§ 3.005. Gifts Between Spouses

If one spouse makes a gift of property to the other spouse, the gift is presumed to include all the income and property that may arise from that property.

SUBTITLE C. DISSOLUTION OF MARRIAGE

CHAPTER 6. SUIT FOR DISSOLUTION OF MARRIAGE

SUBCHAPTER A. GROUNDS FOR DIVORCE AND DEFENSES

§ 6.001. Insupportability

On the petition of either party to a marriage, a divorce may be decreed without regard to fault if the marriage has become insupportable because of discord or conflict of personalities that destroys the legitimate ends of the marriage relationship and prevents any reasonable expectation of reconciliation. [**Author's Note:** The traditional grounds are found in §§6.002 through 6.007.]

SUBCHAPTER D. JURISDICTION, VENUE, AND RESIDENCY QUALIFICATIONS

§ 6.301. General Residency Rule for Divorce Suit

A suit for divorce may not be maintained in this state unless at the time the suit is filed either the petitioner or the respondent has been:

(1) a domiciliary of this state for the preceding six-month period; and

(2) a resident of the county in which the suit is filed for the preceding 90-day period.

§ 6.302. Suit for Divorce by Nonresident Spouse

If one spouse has been a domiciliary of this state for at least the last six months, a spouse domiciled in another state or nation may file a suit for divorce in the county in which the domiciliary spouse resides at the time the petition is filed.

§ 6.303. Absence on Public Service

Time spent by a Texas domiciliary outside this state or outside the county of residence of the domiciliary while in the service of the armed forces or other service of the United States or of this state is considered residence in this state and in that county.

§ 6.304.   **Armed Forces Personnel Not Previously Residents**

A person not previously a resident of this state who is serving in the armed forces of the United States and has been stationed at one or more military installations in this state for at least the last six months and at a military installation in a county of this state for at least the last 90 days is considered to be a Texas domiciliary and a resident of that county for those periods for the purpose of filing suit for dissolution of a marriage.

§ 6.305.   **Acquiring Jurisdiction Over Nonresident Respondent**

(a) If the petitioner in a suit for dissolution of a marriage is a resident or a domiciliary of this state at the time the suit for dissolution is filed, the court may exercise personal jurisdiction over the respondent or over the respondent's personal representative although the respondent is not a resident of this state if:

> (1)   this state is the last marital residence of the petitioner and the respondent and the suit is filed before the second anniversary of the date on which marital residence ended; or
>
> (2)   there is any basis consistent with the constitutions of this state and the United States for the exercise of the personal jurisdiction.

(b) A court acquiring jurisdiction under this section also acquires jurisdiction over the respondent in a suit affecting the parent-child relationship.

SUBCHAPTER E. FILING SUIT

§ 6.401.   **Caption**

(a) Pleadings in a divorce or annulment suit shall be styled "In the Matter of the Marriage of _____ and _____."

§ 6.402.   **Pleadings**

(a) A petition in a suit for dissolution of marriage is sufficient without the necessity of specifying the underlying evidentiary facts if the petition alleges the grounds relied on substantially in the language of the statute.

(b) Allegations of grounds for relief, matters of defense, or facts relied on for temporary relief that are stated in short and plain terms are not subject to special exceptions because of form or sufficiency.

(c) The court shall strike an allegation of evidentiary fact from the pleadings on the motion of a party or on the court's own motion.

§ 6.403.   **Answer**

The respondent is a suit for dissolution of a marriage is not required to answer on oath or affirmation.

§ 6.404.   **Statement on Alternative Dispute Resolution**

(a) A party to a proceeding under this title shall include in the first pleading filed by the party in the proceeding the following statement:

"I AM AWARE THAT IT IS THE POLICY OF THE STATE OF TEXAS TO PROMOTE

THE AMICABLE AND NONJUDICIAL SETTLEMENT OF DISPUTES INVOLVING CHILDREN AND FAMILIES. I AM AWARE OF ALTERNATIVE DISPUTE RESOLUTION METHODS, INCLUDING MEDIATION. WHILE I RECOGNIZE THAT ALTERNATIVE DISPUTE RESOLUTION IS AN ALTERNATIVE TO AND NOT A SUBSTITUTE FOR A TRIAL AND THAT THIS CASE MAY BE TRIED IF IT IS NOT SETTLED, I REPRESENT TO THE COURT THAT I WILL ATTEMPT IN GOOD FAITH TO RESOLVE CONTESTED ISSUES IN THIS CASE BY ALTERNATIVE DISPUTE RESOLUTION WITHOUT THE NECESSITY OF COURT INTERVENTION."

(b) The statement prescribed by Subsection (a) must be prominently displayed in boldfaced type or capital letters or be underlined and be signed by the party.

(c) The statement prescribed by Subsection (a) is not required for:

(1) a pleading in which citation on all respondents entitled to service of citation is requested, issued, and given by publication;

(2) a motion or pleading that seeks a protective order as provided by Chapter 4; or

(3) a special appearance under Rule 120a, Texas Rules of Civil Procedure.

§ 6.405.   Protective Order

(a) The petition in a suit for dissolution of a marriage must state whether a protective order under Chapter 71 is in effect or if an application for a protective order is pending with regard to the parties to the suit.

(b) The petitioner shall attach to the petition a copy of each protective order issued under Chapter 71 in which one of the parties to the suit was the applicant and the other party was the respondent without regard to the date of the order. If a copy of the protective order is not available at the time of filing, the petition must state that a copy of the order will be filed with the court before any hearing.

§ 6.406.   Mandatory Joinder of Suit Affecting Parent-Child Relationship

(a) The petition in a suit for dissolution of a marriage shall state whether there are children born or adopted of the marriage who are under 18 years of age or who are otherwise entitled to support as provided by Chapter 154.

(b) If the parties are parents of a child, as defined by Section 101.003, and the child is not under the continuing jurisdiction of another court as provided by Chapter 155, the suit for dissolution of a marriage must include a suit affecting the parent-child relationship under Title 5.

SUBCHAPTER H. TRIAL AND APPEAL

§ 6.701.   Failure to Answer

In a suit for divorce, the petition may not be taken as confessed if the respondent does not file an answer.

§ 6.702.   Waiting Period

(a) The court may not grant a divorce before the 60th day after the date the suit was filed. A decree rendered in violation of this subsection is not subject to collateral attack.

(b) A waiting period is not required before a court may grant an annulment or declare a marriage void other than as required in civil cases generally.

§ 6.706.   Change of Name

(a) In a decree of divorce or annulment, the court shall change the name of a party specifically requesting the change to a name previously used by the party unless the court states in the decree a reason for denying the change of name.

(b) The court may not deny a change of name solely to keep the last name of family members.

(c) A change of name does not release a person from liability incurred by the person under a previous name or defeat a right the person held under a previous name.

(d) A person whose name is changed under this section may apply for a change of name certificate from the clerk of the court as provided by Section 45.106.

SUBCHAPTER I. REMARRIAGE

§ 6.801.   Remarriage

(a) Except as otherwise provided by this subchapter, neither party to a divorce may marry a third party before the 31st day after the date the divorce is decreed.

(b) The former spouses may marry each other at any time.

§ 6.902.   Waiver of Prohibition Against Remarriage

For good cause shown the court may waive the prohibition against remarriage provided by this subchapter as to either or both spouses if a record of the proceedings is made and preserved or if findings of fact and conclusions of law are filed by the court.

CHAPTER 7. AWARD OF MARITAL PROPERTY

§ 7.001.   General Rule of Property Division

In a decree of divorce or annulment, the court shall order a division of the estate of the parties in a manner that the court deems just and right, having due regard for the rights of each party and any children of the marriage.

§ 7.002   Division of Property Under Special Circumstances

In addition to the division of the estate of the parties required by Section 7.001, in a decree of divorce or annulment the court shall order a division of the following real and personal property, wherever situated, in a manner that the court deems just and right, having due regard for the rights of each party and any children of the marriage:

     (1)   property that was acquired by either spouse while domiciled in another state and that would have been community property if the spouse who acquired the property had been domiciled in this state at the time of the acquisition; or

     (2)   property that was acquired by either spouse in exchange for real or personal property and that would have been community property if the spouse who acquired the property so exchanged had been domiciled in this state at the time of its acquisition.

     (3)   the equitable interest, as provided by Subchapter E, Chapter 3, of the:

          (A) community estate in the separate estate of a spouse;

          (B) separate property of a spouse in the separate property of the other spouse; and

          (C) separate property of a spouse in the community estate.

§ 7.003.   Disposition of Retirement and Employment Benefits and Other Plans

In a decree of divorce or annulment, the court shall determine the rights of both spouses in any pension, retirement plan, annuity, individual retirement account, employee stock option plan, stock option, or other form of savings, bonus, profit-sharing, or other employer plan or financial plan of an employee or a participant, regardless of whether the person is self-employed, in the nature of compensation or savings.

§ 7.004.   Disposition of Rights in Insurance

In a decree of divorce or annulment, the court shall specifically divide or award the rights of each spouse in an insurance policy.

§ 7.005.   Insurance Coverage Not Specifically Awarded

(a) If in a decree of divorce or annulment the court does not specifically award all of the rights of the spouses in an insurance policy other than life insurance in effect at the time the decree is rendered, the policy remains in effect until the policy expires according to the policy's own terms.

(b) The proceeds of a valid claim under the policy are payable as follows:

     (1)   if the interest in the property insured was awarded solely to one former spouse by the decree, to that former spouse;

     (2)   if an interest in the property insured was awarded to each former spouse, to those former spouses in proportion to the interests awarded;

     (3)   if the insurance coverage is directly related to the person of one of the former spouses, to that former spouse.

(c) The failure of either former spouse to change the endorsement on the policy to reflect the distribution of proceeds established by this section does not relieve the insurer of liability to pay the proceeds or any other obligation on the policy.

(d) This section does not affect the right of a former spouse to assert an ownership interest in an undivided life insurance policy, as provided by Subchapter D, Chapter 9.

§ 7.006.   Agreement Incident to Divorce or Annulment

(a) To promote amicable settlement of disputes in a suit for divorce or annulment, the spouses may enter into a written agreement concerning the division of the property and the liabilities of the spouses and maintenance of either spouse. The agreement may be revised or repudiated before rendition of the divorce or annulment unless the agreement is binding under another rule of law.

(b) If the court finds that the terms of the written agreement in a divorce or annulment are just and right, those terms are binding on the court. If the court approves the agreement, the court may set forth the agreement in full or incorporate the agreement by reference in the final decree.

(c) If the court finds that the terms of the written agreement in a divorce or annulment are not just and right, the court may request the spouses to submit a revised agreement or may set the case for a contested hearing.

CHAPTER 8. MAINTENANCE

§ 8.001.   Definition

In this chapter, "maintenance" means an award in a suit for dissolution of marriage of periodic payments from the future income of one spouse for the support of the other spouse.

§ 8.002.   Eligibility for Maintenance

In a suit for dissolution of marriage or in a proceeding for maintenance in a court with personal jurisdiction over both former spouses following the dissolution of their marriage by a court that lacked personal jurisdiction over an absent spouse, the court may order maintenance for either spouse only if:

(1) the spouse from whom maintenance is requested was convicted of or received deferred adjudication for a criminal offense that also constitutes an act of family violence under Chapter 71 and the offense occurred:

(A) within two years before the date on which a suit for dissolution of marriage is filed; or

(B) while the suit is pending; or

(2) the duration of the marriage was 10 years or longer, the spouse seeking maintenance lacks sufficient property, including property distributed to the spouse under this code, to provide for the spouse's minimum reasonable needs, as limited by Section 8.005, and the spouse seeking maintenance:

(A) is unable to support himself or herself through appropriate employment because of an incapacitating physical or mental disability;

(B) is the custodian of a child who requires substantial care and personal supervision because a physical or mental disability makes it necessary, taking into consideration the needs of the child, that the spouse not be employed outside the home; or

(C) clearly lacks earning ability in the labor market adequate to provide support for the spouse's minimum reasonable needs, as limited by Section 8.005.

§ 8.003.   **Factors in Determining Maintenance**

A court that determines that a spouse is eligible to receive maintenance under this chapter shall determine the nature, amount, duration, and manner of periodic payments by considering all relevant factors, including:

(1)   the financial resources of the spouse seeking maintenance, including the community and separate property and liabilities apportioned to that spouse in the dissolution proceeding, and that spouse's ability to meet the spouse's needs independently;

(2)   the education and employment skills of the spouses, the time necessary to acquire sufficient education or training to enable the spouse seeking maintenance to find appropriate employment, the availability of that education or training, and the feasibility of that education or training;

(3)   the duration of the marriage;

(4)   the age, employment history, earning ability, and physical and emotional condition of the spouse seeking maintenance;

(5)   the ability of the spouse from whom maintenance is requested to meet that spouse's personal needs and to provide periodic child support payments, if applicable, while meeting the personal needs of the spouse seeking maintenance;

(6)   acts by either spouse resulting in excessive or abnormal expenditures or destruction, concealment, or fraudulent disposition of community property, joint tenancy, or other property held in common;

(7)   the comparative financial resources of the spouses, including medical, retirement, insurance, or other benefits, and the separate property of each spouse;

(8)   the contribution by one spouse to the education, training, or increased earning power of the other spouse;

(9)   the property brought to the marriage by either spouse;

(10)   the contribution of a spouse as homemaker;

(11)   marital misconduct of the spouse seeking maintenance; and

(12)   the efforts of the spouse seeking maintenance to pursue available employment counseling as provided by Chapter 304, Labor Code.

§ 8.004.   **Presumption**

(a) Except as provided by Subsection (b), it is presumed that maintenance is not warranted unless the spouse seeking maintenance has exercised diligence in:

(1)   seeking suitable employment; or

(2)   developing the necessary skills to become self-supporting during a period of separation and during the time the suit for dissolution of the marriage is pending.

(b) This section does not apply to a spouse who is not able to satisfy the presumption in Subsection (a) because of an incapacitating physical or mental disability

§ 8.005. Duration of Maintenance Order

(a) Except as provided by Subsection (b), a court:

    (1) may not order maintenance that remains in effect for more that three years after the date of the order; and

    (2) shall limit the duration of a maintenance order to the shortest reasonable period that allows the spouse seeking maintenance to meet the spouse's minimum reasonable needs by obtaining appropriate employment or developing an appropriate skill, unless the ability of the spouse to provide for the spouse's minimum reasonable needs through employment is substantially or totally diminished because of:

    (A) physical or mental disability;

    (B) duties as the custodian of an infant or young child; or

    (C) another compelling impediment to gainful employment.

(b) If a spouse seeking maintenance is unable to support himself or herself through appropriate employment because of an incapacitating physical or mental disability, the court may order maintenance for an indefinite period for as long as the disability continues. The court may order the periodic review of its order, on the request of either party or on its own motion, to determine whether the disability is continuing. The continuation of spousal maintenance under these circumstances is subject to a motion to modify as provided by Section 8.008.

§ 8.006. Amount of Maintenance

(a) A court may not order maintenance that requires a spouse to pay monthly more than the lesser of:

    (1) $2,500; or

    (2) 20 percent of the spouse's average monthly gross income.

(b) The court shall set the amount that a spouse is required to pay in a maintenance order to provide for the minimum reasonable needs of the spouse receiving the maintenance under the order, considering employment or property received in the dissolution of the marriage or otherwise owned by the spouse receiving the maintenance that contributes to the minimum needs of that spouse.

(c) Department of Veterans Affairs service-connected disability compensation, social security benefits and disability benefits, and workers' compensation benefits are excluded from maintenance.

§ 8.007. Termination

(a) The obligation to pay future maintenance terminates on the death of either party or on the remarriage of the party receiving maintenance.

(b) After a hearing, the court shall terminate the maintenance order if the party receiving maintenance cohabits with another person in a permanent place of abode on a continuing, conjugal basis.

CHAPTER 102

§ 102.008.   Contents of Petition [Author's Note: This relates to the situation where there are minor children]

(a)   The petition and all other documents in a proceeding filed under this title (except a suit for adoption of an adult) shall be entitled "In the interest of _____, a child."

(b)   The petition must include:

(1)   a statement that the court in which the petition is filed has continuing exclusive jurisdiction or that no court has continuing jurisdiction of the suit;

(2)   the name, sex, place and date of birth, and place of residence of the child, except that if adoption of a child is requested, the name of the child may be omitted;

(3)   the full name, age, and place of residence of the petitioner and the petitioner's relationship to the child or the fact that no relationship exists;

(4)   the names, ages, and place of residence of the parents, except in a suit in which adoption is requested;

(5)   the name and place of residence of the managing conservator, if any, or the child's custodian, if any, appointed by an order of the court another state or country;

(6)   the names and places of residence or the guardians of the person and estate of the child, if any;

(7)   the names and places of residence of possessory conservators or other persons, if any, having possession of or access to the child under an order of the court;

(8)   the name and place of residence of the alleged father of the child or a statement that the identity of the father of the child is unknown;

(9)   a full description and statement of value of all property owned or possessed by the child;

(10)   a statement describing what action the court is requested to make concerning the child and the statutory grounds on which the request is made; and

(11)   any other information required by this title.

§ 102.0085.   Statement on Alternative Dispute Resolution

(a)   A party to a proceeding brought under this chapter and Chapters 151, 153, 154, and 160 shall include in the first pleading filed by the party in the proceeding the following statement:

"I AM AWARE THAT IT IS THE POLICY OF THE STATE OF TEXAS TO PROMOTE THE AMICABLE AND NONJUDICIAL SETTLEMENT OF DISPUTES INVOLVING CHILDREN AND FAMILIES. I AM AWARE OF ALTERNATIVE DISPUTE RESOLUTION METHODS INCLUDING MEDIATION. WHILE I RECOGNIZE THAT ALTERNATIVE DISPUTE RESOLUTION IS AN ALTERNATIVE TO AND NOT A SUBSTITUTE FOR A TRIAL AND THAT THIS CASE MAY BE TRIED IF IT IS NOT SETTLED, I REPRESENT TO THE COURT THAT I WILL ATTEMPT IN GOOD FAITH TO RESOLVE CONTESTED ISSUES IN THIS CASE BY ALTERNATIVE DISPUTE RESOLUTION WITHOUT THE NECESSITY OF COURT INTERVENTION."

(b)   The statement required by Subsection (a) must be prominently displayed in boldface type or capital letters or be underlined and be signed by the party.

(c)   The statement in Subsection (a) is not required for:

(1) a pleading in which citation on all respondents entitled to service of citation is requested, issued, and given by publication;

(2) a motion or pleading that seeks relief under Section 105.001(c) or Subchapter H, Chapter 157; or

(3) a special appearance under Rule 120A, Texas Rules of Civil Procedure.

CHAPTER 105

§ 105.006. Contents of Final Order

(a) A final order must contain:

(1) the social security number and driver's license number of each party to the suit, including the child, except that the child's social security number or driver's license number is not required if the child has not been assigned a social security number or driver's license number; and

(2) each party's current residence address, mailing address, home telephone number, name of employer, address of employment, and work telephone number, except as provided by Subsection (c).

(b) Except as provided by Subsection (c), the court shall order each party to inform each other party of an intended change in any of the information required by this section as long as any person, as a result of the order, is under an obligation to pay child support or is entitled to possession of or access to a child. The court shall order that notice of the intended change be given at the earlier of:

(1) the 60th day before the date the party intends to make the change; or

(2) the fifth day after the date that the party knew of the change, if the party did not know or could not have known of the change in sufficient time to comply with Subdivision (1).

(c) If a court finds after notice and hearing that requiring a party to provide the information required by this section is likely to cause the child or a conservator harassment, abuse, serious harm, or injury, the court may:

(1) order the information not to be disclosed to another party; or

(2) render any other order the court considers necessary.

(d) An order in a suit that orders child support or possession of or access to a child must contain the following notice in bold-faced type or in capital letters:

"FAILURE TO OBEY A COURT ORDER FOR CHILD SUPPORT OR FOR POSSESSION OF OR ACCESS TO A CHILD MAY RESULT IN FURTHER LITIGATION TO ENFORCE THE ORDER, INCLUDING CONTEMPT OF COURT. A FINDING OF CONTEMPT MAY BE PUNISHED BY CONFINEMENT IN JAIL FOR UP TO SIX MONTHS, A FINE OF UP TO $500 FOR EACH VIOLATION, AND A MONEY JUDGMENT FOR PAYMENT OF ATTORNEY'S FEES AND COURT COSTS.

"FAILURE OF A PARTY TO MAKE A CHILD SUPPORT PAYMENT TO THE PLACE AND IN THE MANNER REQUIRED BY A COURT ORDER MAY RESULT IN THE PARTY NOT RECEIVING CREDIT FOR MAKING THE PAYMENT.

"FAILURE OF A PARTY TO PAY CHILD SUPPORT DOES NOT JUSTIFY DENYING THAT PARTY COURT-ORDERED POSSESSION OF OR ACCESS TO A CHILD. REFUSAL BY A PARTY TO ALLOW POSSESSION OF OR ACCESS TO A CHILD DOES NOT JUSTIFY FAILURE TO PAY COURT-ORDERED CHILD SUPPORT TO THAT PARTY."

(e) Except as provided by Subsection (c), an order in a suit that orders child support or possession of or access to a child must also contain the following order in bold-faced type or in capital letters:

"EACH PERSON WHO IS A PARTY TO THIS ORDER IS ORDERED TO NOTIFY EACH OTHER PARTY WITHIN 10 DAYS AFTER THE DATE OF ANY CHANGE IN THE PARTY'S CURRENT RESIDENCE ADDRESS, MAILING ADDRESS, HOME TELEPHONE NUMBER, NAME OF EMPLOYER, ADDRESS OF EMPLOYMENT, AND WORK TELEPHONE NUMBER. THE PARTY IS ORDERED TO GIVE NOTICE OF AN INTENDED CHANGE IN ANY OF THE REQUIRED INFORMATION TO EACH OTHER PARTY ON OR BEFORE THE 60TH DAY BEFORE THE INTENDED CHANGE. IF THE PARTY DOES NOT KNOW OR COULD NOT HAVE KNOWN OF THE CHANGE IN SUFFICIENT TIME TO PROVIDE 60-DAY NOTICE, THE PARTY IS ORDERED TO GIVE NOTICE OF THE CHANGE ON OR BEFORE THE FIFTH DAY AFTER THE DATE THAT THE PARTY KNOWS OF THE CHANGE.

"THE DUTY TO FURNISH THIS INFORMATION TO EACH OTHER PARTY CONTINUES AS LONG AS ANY PERSON, BY VIRTUE OF THIS ORDER, IS UNDER AN OBLIGATION TO PAY CHILD SUPPORT OR IS ENTITLED TO POSSESSION OF OR ACCESS TO A CHILD.

"FAILURE BY A PARTY TO OBEY THE ORDER OF THIS COURT TO PROVIDE EACH OTHER PARTY WITH THE CHANGE IN THE REQUIRED INFORMATION MAY RESULT IN FURTHER LITIGATION TO ENFORCE THE ORDER, INCLUDING CONTEMPT OF COURT. A FINDING OF CONTEMPT MAY BE PUNISHED BY CONFINEMENT IN JAIL FOR UP TO SIX MONTHS, A FINE OF UP TO $500 FOR EACH VIOLATION, AND A MONEY JUDGMENT FOR PAYMENT OF ATTORNEY'S FEES AND COURT COSTS."

CHAPTER 153

SUBCHAPTER A. GENERAL PROVISIONS

§ 153.001. **Public Policy**
 (a) The public policy of this state is to:
  (1) assure that children will have frequent and continuing contact with parents who have shown the ability to act in the best interest of the child;
  (2) provide a safe, stable, and nonviolent environment for the child; and
  (3) encourage parents to share in the rights and duties of raising their child after the parents have separated or dissolved their marriage.
 (b) A court may not render an order that conditions the right of a conservator to possession of or access to a child on the payment of child support.

§ 153.002. Best Interest of Child

The best interest of the child shall always be the primary consideration of the court in determining the issues of conservatorship and possession of and access to the child.

§ 153.002. No Discrimination Based on Sex or Marital Status

The court shall consider the qualifications of the parties without regard to their marital status or to the sex of the party or the child in determining:

(1) which party to appoint as sole managing conservator;

(2) whether to appoint a party as joint managing conservator; and

(3) the terms and conditions of conservatorship and possession of and access to the child.

§ 153.004. History of Domestic Violence

(a) In determining whether to appoint a party as a sole or joint managing conservator, the court shall consider evidence of the intentional use of abusive physical force by a party against the party's spouse, a parent of the child, or any person younger than 18 years of age committed within a two-year period preceding the filing of the suit or during the pendency of the suit.

(b) The court may not appoint joint managing conservators if credible evidence is presented of a history or pattern of past or present child neglect, or physical or sexual abuse by one parent directed against the other parent, a spouse, or a child.

(c) The court shall consider the commission of family violence in determining whether to deny, restrict, or limit the possession of a child by a parent who is appointed as a possessory conservator.

(d) [HB 1411] The court may not allow a parent to have access to a child for whom it is shown by a preponderance of the evidence that there is a history or pattern of committing family violence during the two years preceding the date of the filing of the suit or during the pendency of the suit, unless the court:

(1) finds that awarding the parent access to the child would not endanger the child's physical health or emotional welfare and would be in the best interest of the child; and

(2) renders a possession order that is designed to protect the safety and well-being of the child and any other person who has been a victim of family violence committed to the parent and that may include a requirement that:

(A) the periods of access be continuously supervised by an entity or person chosen by the court;

(B) the exchange of possession of the child occur in a protective setting;

(C) the parent abstain from the consumption of alcohol or a controlled substance, as defined by Chapter 481, Health and Safety Code, within 12 hours prior to or during the period of access to the child; or

(D) the parent attend and complete a battering intervention and prevention program as provided by Article 42.141, Code of Criminal Procedure, or, if such a program is not available, complete a course of treatment under Section 153.010.

§ 153.005. Appointment of Sole or Joint Managing Conservator

(a) In a suit, the court may appoint a sole managing conservator or may appoint joint managing conservators. If the parents are or will be separated, the court shall appoint at least one managing conservator.

(b) A managing conservator must be a parent, a competent adult, an authorized agency, or a licensed child-placing agency.

§ 153.007. Agreement Concerning Conservatorship

(a) To promote the amicable settlement of disputes between the parties to a suit, the parties may enter into a written agreement containing provisions for conservatorship and possession of the child and for modification of the agreement, including variations from the standard possession order.

(b) If the court finds that the agreement is in the child's best interest, the court shall render an order in accordance with the agreement.

(c) Terms of the agreement contained in the order or incorporated by reference regarding conservatorship or support of or access to a child in an order may be enforced by all remedies available for enforcement of a judgment, including contempt, but are not enforceable as a contract.

(d) If the court finds the agreement is not in the child's best interest, the court may request the parties to submit a revised agreement or the court may render an order for the conservatorship and possession of the child.

§ 153.008. Child's Choice of Managing Conservator

If the child is 10 years of age or older, the child may, by writing filed with the court, choose the managing conservator, subject to the approval of the court.

§ 153.009. Interview of Child in Chambers

(a) In a nonjury trial the court may interview the child in chambers to determine the child's wishes as to conservatorship.

(b) When the issue of managing conservatorship is contested, on the application of a party, the court shall interview a child 12 years of age or older and may interview a child under 12 years of age. Interviewing a child does not diminish the discretion of the court.

(c) The court may permit the attorney for a party or the attorney ad litem for the child to be present at the interview.

(d) On motion of a party or on the court's own motion, the court shall cause a record of the interview to be made when the child is 12 years of age or older. A record of the interview shall be part of the record in the case.

§ 153.073. Rights of Parent at All Times

(a) Unless limited by court, a parent appointed as a conservator of a child has at all times the right:

    (1) as specified by court order;

        (A) to receive information from the other parent concerning the health, education, and welfare of the child; and

    (B) to confer with the other parent to the extent possible before making a decision concerning the health, education, and welfare of the child;

  (2) of access to medical, dental, psychological, and educational records of the child;

  (3) to consult with a physician, dentist, or psychologist of the child;

  (4) to consult with school officials concerning the child's welfare and educational status, including school activities;

  (5) to attend school activities;

  (6) to be designated on the child's records as a person to be notified in case of an emergency;

  (7) to consent to medical, dental, and surgical treatment during an emergency involving an immediate danger to the health and safety of the child; and

  (8) to manage the estate of the child to the extent the estate has been created by the parent or the parent's family.

  (b) The court shall specify in the order the rights that a parent retains at all times.

§ 153.074. Rights and Duties During Period of Possession

Unless limited by court order, a parent appointed as a conservator of a child has the following rights and duties during the period that the parent has possession of the child:

  (1) the duty of care, control, protection, and reasonable discipline of the child;

  (2) the duty to support the child, including providing the child with clothing, food, shelter, and medical and dental care not involving an invasive procedure;

  (3) the right to consent for the child to medical and dental care not involving an invasive procedure;

  (4) the right to consent for the child to medical, dental, and surgical treatment during an emergency involving immediate danger to the health and safety of the child; and

  (5) the right to direct the moral and religious training of the child.

§ 153.076. Parents' Duty to Provide Information

  (a) If both parents are appointed as conservators of the child, the court shall order that each parent has a duty to inform the other parent in a timely manner of significant information concerning the health, education, and welfare of the child.

  (b) If both parents are appointed as conservators of a child, the court shall order that each parent has the duty to inform the other parent if the parent if the parent resides with for at least 30 days, marries, or intends to marry a person who the parent knows:

    (1) is registered as a sex offender under Chapter 62, Code of Criminal Procedures, as added by Chapter 668, Acts of the 75th Legislature, Regular Session, 1997; or

    (2) is currently charged with an offense for which on conviction the person would be required to register under that chapter.

  (c) The notice required to be made under Subsection (b) must be made as soon practicable but not later that the 40th day after the date the parent begins to reside with the person or the 10th day after the date the marriage occurs as appropriate. The notice must include a description of the offense that is the basis of the person's requirement to register as a sex offender or of the offense with which the person is charged.

(d) A person commits an offense if the person fails to provide notice in the manner required by Subsections (b) and (c). An offense under this subsection is a Class C misdemeanor.

SUBCHAPTER C. PARENT APPOINTED AS SOLE OR JOINT MANAGING CONSERVATOR

§ 153.131. Presumption that Parent to be Appointed Managing Conservator
(a) Unless the court finds that appointment of the parent or parents would not be in the best interest of the child because the appointment would significantly impair the child's physical health or emotional development, a parent shall be appointed sole managing conservator or both parents shall be appointed as joint managing conservators of the child.

(b) It is a rebuttable presumption that the appointment of the parents of a child as joint managing conservators is in the best interest of the child.

§ 153.132. Rights and Duties of Parent Appointed Sole Managing Conservator
Unless limited by court order, a parent appointed as sole managing conservator of a child has the rights and duties provided in Subchapter B and the following exclusive rights:
   (1) the right to establish the primary residence of the child;
   (2) the right to consent to medical, dental, and surgical treatment involving invasive procedures, and to consent to psychiatric and psychological treatment;
   (3) the right to receive and give receipt for periodic payments for the support of the child and to hold or disburse these funds for the benefit of the child;
   (4) the right to represent the child in legal action and to make other decisions of substantial legal significance concerning the child;
   (5) the right to consent to marriage and to enlistment in the armed forces of the United States;
   (6) the right to make decisions concerning the child's education;
   (7) the right to the services and earnings of the child; and
   (8) except when a guardian of the child's estate or a guardian or attorney ad litem has been appointed for the child, the right to act as an agent of the child in relation to the child's estate if the child's action is required by a state, the United States, or a foreign government.

§ 153.133. Agreement for Joint Managing Conservatorship
(a) If a written agreement of the parents is filed with the court, the court shall render an order appointing the parents as joint managing conservators only if the agreement:
   (1) designates the conservator who has the exclusive right to establish the primary residence of the child and:
      (A) establishes, until modified by further order, the geographic area within which the conservator shall maintain the child's primary residence; or
      (B) specifies that the conservator may establish the child's primary residence without regard to geographic location;
   (2) specifies the rights and duties of each parent regarding the child's physical care, support, and education;

    (3) includes provisions to minimize disruption of the child's education, daily routine, and association with friends;

    (4) allocates between the parents, independently, jointly, or exclusively, all of the remaining rights and duties of a parent provided by Chapter 151;

    (5) is voluntarily and knowingly made by each parent and has not been repudiated by either parent at the time the order is rendered; and

    (6) is in the best interest of the child.

§ 153.134. Court-Ordered Joint Conservatorship

    (a) If a written agreement of the parents is not filed with the court, the court may render an order appointing the parents joint managing conservators only if the appointment is in the best interest of the child, considering the following factors:

    (1) whether the physical, psychological, or emotional needs and development of the child will benefit from the appointment of joint managing conservators;

    (2) the ability of the parents to give first priority to the welfare of the child and reach shared decisions in the child's best interest;

    (3) whether each parent can encourage and accept a positive relationship between the child and the other parent;

    (4) whether both parents participated in child rearing before the filing of the suit;

    (5) the geographical proximity of the parents' residences;

    (6) if the child is 12 years of age or older, the child's preference, if any, regarding the appointment of joint managing conservators; and

    (7) any other relevant factor.

    (b) In rendering an order appointing joint managing conservators, the court shall:

    (1) designates the conservator who has the exclusive right to determine the primary residence of the child and:

    (A) establish, until modified by further order, the geographic area consisting of the county in which the child is to reside and any contiguous county thereto within which the conservator shall maintain the child's primary residence; or

    (B) specify that the conservator may determine the child's primary residence without regard to geographic location;

    (2) specify the rights and duties of each parent regarding the child's physical care, support, and education;

    (3) include provisions to minimize disruption of the child's education, daily routine, and association with friends;

    (4) allocate between the parents, independently, jointly, or exclusively, all of the remaining rights and duties of a parent as provided by Chapter 151 and;

    (5) if feasible, recommend that the parties use an alternative dispute resolution method before requesting enforcement or modification of the terms and conditions of the joint conservatorship through litigation, except in an emergency.

§ 153.254. Child Less Than Three Years of Age

    (a) The court shall render an order appropriate under the circumstances for possession of a child less than three years of age.

    (b) The court shall render a prospective order to take effect on the child's third birthday, which presumptively will be the standard possession order.

§ 153.256. Factors for Court to Consider

In ordering the terms of possession of a child under an order other than a standard possession order, the court shall be guided by the guidelines established by the standard possession order and may consider:

(1) the age, developmental status, circumstances, needs, and best interest of the child;

(2) the circumstances of the managing conservator and of the parent named as a possessory conservator; and

(3) any other relevant factor.

SUBCHAPTER F. STANDARD POSSESSION ORDER

§ 153.311. Mutual Agreement or Specified Terms for Possession

The court shall specify in a standard possession order that the parties may have possession of the child at times mutually agreed to in advance by the parties and, in the absence of mutual agreement, shall have possession of the child under the specified terms set out in the standard order.

§ 153.312. Parents Who Reside 100 miles or Less Apart

(a) If the possessory conservator resides 100 miles or less from the primary residence of the child, the possessory conservator shall have the right to possession of the child as follows:

(1) on weekends beginning at 6 p.m. on the first, third, and fifth Friday of each month and ending at 6 p.m. on the following Sunday or, at the possessory conservator's election made before or at the time of the rendition of the original or modification order, and as specified in the original or modification order, beginning at the time the child's school is regularly dismissed and ending at 6 p.m. on the following Sunday; and

(2) on Wednesdays of each week during the regular school term beginning at 6 p.m. and ending at 8 p.m., or, at the possessory conservator's election made before or at the time of the rendition of the original or modification order, and as specified in the original or modification order, beginning at the time the child's school is regularly dismissed and ending at the time the child's school resumes, unless the court finds that visitation under this subdivision is not in the best interest of the child.

(b) The following provisions govern possession of the child for vacations and certain specific holidays and supersede conflicting weekend or Wednesday periods of possession. The possessory conservator and the managing conservator shall have rights of possession of the child as follows:

(1) the possessory conservator shall have possession in even-numbered years, beginning at 6 p.m. on the day the child is dismissed from school for the school's spring vacation and ending at 6 p.m. on the day before school resumes after that vacation, and the managing conservator shall have possession for the same period in odd-numbered years;

(2) if a possessory conservator:

(A) gives the managing conservator written notice by April 1 of each year specifying an extended period or periods of summer possession, the possessory conservator shall have possession of the child for 30 days beginning not earlier than the day after the child's school is dismissed for the summer vacation and ending no later than seven days before school resumes at the end of the summer vacation, to be exercised in not more than two separate periods of at least seven consecutive days each; or

(B) does not give the managing conservator written notice by April 1 of each year specifying an extended period or periods of summer possession, the possessory conservator shall have possession of the child for 30 connective days beginning at 6 p.m. on July 1 and ending at 6 p.m. on July 31;

(3) if the managing conservator gives the possessory conservator written notice by April 15 of each year, the managing conservator shall have possession of the child on any one weekend beginning Friday at 6 p.m. and ending at 6 p.m. on the following Sunday during one period of possession by the possessory conservator under Subdivision (2), provided that the managing conservator picks up the child from the possessory conservator and returns the child to that same place; and

(4) if the managing conservator gives the possessory conservator written notice by April 15 of each year or gives the possessory conservator 14 days' written notice on or after April 16 of each year, the managing conservator may designate one weekend beginning not earlier than the day after the child's school is dismissed for the summer vacation and ending not later than seven days before school resuming at the end of the summer vacation, during which an otherwise scheduled weekend period of possession by the possessory conservator will not take place, provided that the weekend designated does not interfere with the possessory conservator's period or periods of extended summer possession or with Father's Day if the possessory conservator is the father of the child.

§ 153.313.   Parents Who Reside Over 100 Miles Apart

If the possessory conservator resides more than 100 miles from the residence of the child, the possessory conservator shall have the right to possession of the child as follows:

(1) either regular weekend possession beginning on the first, third, and fifth Friday as provided under the terms applicable to parents who reside 100 miles or less apart or not more than one weekend per month of the possessory conservator's choice beginning at 6 p.m. on the day school recesses for the weekend and ending at 6 p.m. on the day before school resumes after the weekend, provided that the possessory conservator gives the managing conservator 14 days' written or telephonic notice preceding a designated weekend, and provided that the possessory conservator elects an option for this alternative period of possession by written notice given to the managing conservator within 90 days after the parties begin to reside more than 100 miles apart, as applicable;

(2) each year beginning on the day the child is dismissed from school for the school's spring vacation and ending at 6 p.m. on the day before school resumes after that vacation;

(3) if the possessory conservator:

    (A) gives the managing conservator written notice by April 1 of each year specifying an extended period or periods of summer possession, the possessory conservator shall have possession of the child for 42 days beginning not earlier than the day after the child's school is dismissed for the summer vacation and ending not later than seven days before school resumes at the end of the summer vacation, to be exercised in not more than two separate periods of at least seven consecutive days each; or

    (B) does not give the managing conservator written notice by April 1 of each year specifying an extended period or periods of summer possession, the possessory conservator shall have possession of the child for 42 consecutive days beginning at 6 p.m. on June 15 and ending at 6 p.m. on July 27;

(4) if the managing conservator gives the possessory conservator written notice by April 15 of each year the managing conservator shall have possession of the child on one weekend beginning at Friday at 6 p.m. and ending at 6 p.m. on the following Sunday during one period of possession by the possessory conservator under Subdivision (3), provided that if a period of possession by the possessory conservator exceeds 30 days, the managing conservator may have possession of the child under the terms of this subdivision on two nonconsecutive weekends during that time period, and further provided that the managing conservator picks up the child from the possessory conservator and returns the child to that same place; and

(5) if the managing conservator gives the possessory conservator written notice by April 15 of each year, the managing conservator may designate 21 days beginning not earlier than the day after the child's school is dismissed for the summer vacation and ending not later than seven days before school resumes at the end of the summer vacation, to be exercised in not more than two separate periods of at least seven consecutive days each, during which the possessory conservator may not have possession of the child, provided that the period or periods so designated do not interfere with the possessory conservator's periods or periods of extended summer possession or with Father's Day if the possessory conservator is the father of the child.

§ 153.314. Holiday Possession Unaffected by Distance Parents Reside Apart

The following provisions govern possession of the child for certain specific holidays and supersede conflicting weekend or Wednesday periods of possession without regard to the distance the parents reside apart. The possessory conservator and the managing conservator shall have rights of possession of the child as follows:

(1) the possessory conservator shall have possession of the child in even-numbered years beginning at 6 p.m. on the day the child is dismissed from school for the Christmas school vacation and ending at noon on December 26, and the managing conservator shall have possession for the same period in odd-numbered years;

(2) the possessory conservator shall have possession of the child in odd-numbered years beginning at noon on December 26 and ending at 6 p.m. on the day

before school resumes after that vacation, and the managing conservator shall have possession for the same period in even-numbered years;

(3) the possessory conservator shall have possession of the child in odd-numbered years, beginning at 6 p.m. on the day the child is dismissed from school before Thanksgiving and ending at 6 p.m. on the following Sunday, and the managing conservator shall have possession for the same period in even-numbered years;

(4) the parent not otherwise entitled under this standard order to present possession of a child on the child's birthday shall have possession of the child beginning at 6 p.m. and ending at 8 p.m. on that day, provided that the parent picks up the child from the residence of the conservator entitled to possession and returns the child to that same place;

(5) if a conservator, the father shall have possession of the child beginning at 6 p.m. on the Friday preceding Father's Day and ending on Father's Day at 6 p.m., provided that, if he is not otherwise entitled under this standard order to present possession of the child, he picks up the child from the residence of the conservator entitled to possession and returns the child to that same place; and

(6) if a conservator, the mother shall have possession of the child beginning at 6 p.m. on the Friday preceding Mother's Day and ending on Mother's Day at 6 p.m., provided that, if she is not otherwise entitled under this standard order to present possession of the child, she picks up the child from the residence of the conservator entitled to possession and returns the child to that same place.

§ 153.315.　Weekend Possession Extended by Holiday

(a) If a weekend period of possession of the possessory conservator coincides with a school holiday during regular school term or with a federal, state, or local holiday during the summer months in which school is not in session, the weekend possession shall end at 6 p.m. on a Monday holiday or school holiday or shall begin at 6 p.m. Thursday for a Friday holiday or school holiday, as applicable.

(b) At the possessory conservator's election, made before or at the time of the rendition of the original or modification order, and as specified in the original or modification order, periods of possession extended by a holiday may begin at the time the child's school is regularly dismissed.

§ 153.316.　General Terms and Conditions

The court shall order the following general terms and conditions of possession of a child to apply without regard to the distance between the residence of a parent and the child:

(1) the managing conservator shall surrender the child to the possessory conservator at the beginning of each period of the possessory conservator's possession at the residence of the managing conservator;

(2) if the possessory conservator elects to begin a period of possession at the time the child's school is regularly dismissed, the managing conservator shall surrender the child to the possessory conservator at the beginning of each period of possession at the school in which the child is enrolled;

(3) the possessory conservator shall be ordered to do one of the following:

(A) the possessory conservator shall surrender the child to the managing conservator at the end of each period of possession at the residence of the possessory conservator; or

(B) the possessory conservator shall return the child to the residence of the managing conservator at the end of each period of possession, except that the order shall provide that if the possessory conservator shall surrender the child to the managing conservator at the end of each period of possession at the residence of the possessory conservator if:

    (i) at the time the original order or a modification of an order establishing terms and conditions of possession or access the possessory conservator and the managing conservator lived in the same county, the possessory conservator's county of residence remains the same after the rendition of the order, and the managing conservator's county of residence changes, effective on the date of the change of residence by the managing conservator; or

    (ii) the possessory conservator and managing conservator lived in the same residence at any time during a six-month period preceding the date on which a suit for dissolution of the marriage was filed and the possessory conservator's county of residence remains the same and the managing conservator's county of residence changes after they no longer live in the same residence, effective on the date the order is rendered;

(4) if the possessory conservator elects to end a period of possession at the time the child's school resumes, the possessory conservator shall surrender the child to the managing conservator at the end of each period of possession at the school in which the child is enrolled;

(5) each conservator shall return with the child the personal effects that the child brought at the beginning of the period of possession;

(6) either parent may designate a competent adult to pick up and return the child, as applicable; a parent or a designated competent adult shall be present when the child is picked up or returned;

(7) a parent shall give notice to the person in possession of the child on each occasion that the parent will be unable to exercise that parent's right of possession for any specified period;

(8) written notice shall be deemed to have been timely made if received or postmarked before or at the time that notice is due; and

(9) if a conservator's time of possession of a child ends at the time school resumes and for any reason the child is not or will not be returned to school, the conservator in possession of the child shall immediately notify the school and the other conservator that the child will not be or has not been returned to school.

§ 153.317. Alternative Possession Times

If a child is enrolled in school and the possessory conservator elects before or at the time of the rendition of the original or modification order, the standard order may expressly provide that the possessory conservator's period of possession shall begin or end, or both, at a different time expressly set in the standard order under and within the range of alternative times provided by one or both of the following subdivisions:

    (1)   instead of a period of possession by a possessory conservator beginning at 6 p.m. on the day school recesses, the period of possession may be set in the standard possession order to begin at the time the child's school is regularly dismissed or at any time between the time the child's school is regularly dismissed and 6 p.m.; and

    (2)   except for Wednesday evening possession, instead of a period of possession by a possessory conservator ending at 6 p.m. on the day before school resumes, the period of possession may be set in the standard order to end at the time school resumes.

CHAPTER 154

SUBCHAPTER B. COMPUTING NET RESOURCES AVAILABLE FOR PAYMENT OF CHILD SUPPORT

§ 154.061   **Computing Net Monthly Income**

OFFICE OF THE ATTORNEY GENERAL 1996 TAX CHARTS

Pursuant to Section 154.061(b) of the Texas Family Code, the Attorney General of Texas as the "agency charged with enforcing child support orders under Part D of Title IV of the federal Social Security Act" has promulgated the following charts to assist courts in establishing the amount of a child support order. These tax charts are applicable to employed and self-employed persons in computing net monthly income.

INSTRUCTIONS FOR USE

To use these tables, first compute the obligator's annual gross income. Then recompute to determine the obligator's average monthly gross income. These tables provide a method for calculating "monthly net income" for child support purposes, subtracting from monthly gross income the social security taxes and the federal income tax withholding for a single person claiming one personal exemption and the standard deduction.

Thereafter, in many cases the guidelines call for a number of additional steps to complete the necessary calculations. For example, Sections 154.061 through 154.068 provide for appropriate additions to "income" as that term is defined for federal income tax purposes, and for certain subtractions from monthly net income, in order to arrive at the net resources of the obligor available for child support purposes. Computation of the obligee's net resources should follow similar steps.

EMPLOYED PERSON
1996 TAX CHART
Social Security Taxes

Monthly Gross Wages	Old-Age Survivors and Disability Insurance Taxes (6.2%)*	Hospital(Medicare) Insurance Taxes (1.45%)*	Federal Income Taxes**	Net Monthly Income
100.00	6.20	1.45	-0-	92.35
200.00	12.40	2.90	-0-	184.70
300.00	18.60	4.35	-0-	277.05
400.00	24.80	5.80	-0-	369.40
500.00	31.00	7.25	-0-	461.75
600.00	37.20	8.70	8.13	545.97
700.00	43.40	10.15	23.13	623.32
800.00	49.60	11.60	38.13	700.67
900.00	55.80	13.05	53.13	778.02
1,000.00	62.00	14.50	68.13	855.37
1,100.00	68.20	15.95	83.13	932.72
1,200.00	74.40	17.40	98.13	1,010.07
1,300.00	80.60	18.85	113.13	1,087.77
1,400.00	86.80	20.30	128.13	1,164.52
1,500.00	93.00	21.75	143.13	1,242.12
1,600.00	99.20	23.20	158.13	1,319.47
1,700.00	105.40	24.65	173.13	1,396.82
1,800.00	111.60	26.10	188.13	1,474.17
1,900.00	117.80	27.55	203.13	1,551.52
2,000.00	124.00	29.00	218.13	1,628.87
2,100.00	130.20	30.45	233.13	1,706.22
2,200.00	136.40	31.90	248.13	1,783.57
2,300.00	142.60	33.35	263.13	1,860.92
2,400.00	148.80	34.80	291.42	1,924.98
2,500.00	155.00	36.25	293.13	2,015.62
2,600.00	161.20	37.70	315.17	2,085.93
2,700.00	167.40	39.15	343.17	2,150.28
2,800.00	173.60	40.60	371.17	2,214.63
2,900.00	179.80	42.05	399.17	2,278.98
3,000.00	186.00	43.50	427.17	2,343.33
3,100.00	192.20	44.95	455.17	2,407.68
3,200.00	198.40	46.40	483.17	2,472.03
3,300.00	204.60	47.85	511.17	2,536.38
3,400.00	210.80	49.30	539.17	2,600.73
3,500.00	217.00	50.75	567.17	2,665.08

Monthly Gross Wages	Old-Age Survivor and Disability Insurance Taxes (6.2%)*	Hospital(Medicare) Insurance Taxes (1.45%)*	Federal Income Taxes**	Net Monthly Income
3,600.00	223.20	52.20	595.17	2,697.18
3,700.00	229.40	53.65	623.17	2,793.78
3,800.00	235.60	55.10	651.17	2,858.13
3,900.00	241.80	56.55	679.17	2,922.48
4,000.00	248.00	58.00	707.17	2,986.83
4,250.00	263.50	61.63	777.17	3,147.70
4,500.00	279.00	65.25	847.17	3,308.58
4,750.00	294.50	68.88	917.17	3,469.45
5,000.00	310.00	72.50	987.17	3,630.33
5,250.00	323.95***	76.13	1,057.17	3,792.75
5,500.00	323.95	79.75	1,130.42	3,965.88
5,750.00	323.95	83.38	1,207.92	4,134.75
6,000.00	323.95	87.00	1,285.42	4,303.63
6,250.00	323.95	90.63	1,362.92	4,472.50
6,500.00	323.95	94.25	1,440.42	4,641.38
6,750.00	323.95	97.88	1,517.92	4,810.25
7,000.00	323.95	101.50	1,595.42	4,979.13
7,500.00	323.95	108.75	1,750.42	5,316.88
8,000.00	323.95	116.00	1,905.42	5,654.63
8,500.00	323.95	123.25	2,060.42	5,992.38
9,000.00	323.95	130.50	2,215.42	6,330.13
9,500.00	323.95	130.75	2,370.42	6,667.88
10,000.00	323.95	145.00	2,526.73	7,004.32
10,500.00	323.95	152.25	2,685.69	7,338.11
11,000.00	323.95	159.60	2,861.89	7,654.66
11,500.00	323.95	166.75	3,046.48	7,962.82
12,000.00	323.95	174.00	3,229.54	8,272.51
12,500.00	323.95	181.25	3,412.60	8,582.20
13,000.00	323.95	188.50	3,597.19	8,890.36

Footnotes to Employed Persons 1996 Tax Chart:

* An employed person not subject to the Old-Age, Survivors and Disability Insurance/Hospital (Medicare) Insurance taxes will be allowed the reductions reflected in these columns, unless it is shown that such person has no similar contributory plan such as teacher retirement, federal railroad retirement, federal civil service retirement, etc.

** These amounts represent one-twelfth (1/12) of the annual Federal income tax calculated for a single taxpayer claiming one person exemption ($2,550.00, subject to reduction in certain cases, as described in the next paragraph of this footnote) and taking the standard deduction ($4,000.00).

For a single taxpayer with an adjusted gross income in excess of $117,950.00, the deduction for the personal exemption is reduced by two percent (2%) for each $2,500.00 or fraction thereof by which adjusted gross income exceeds $117,950.00. The reduction is completed (i.e., the deduction for the personal exemption is eliminated) for adjusted gross income in excess of $240,450.00. In no case is the deduction for the personal exemption reduced by more than 100%. For example, monthly gross wages of $12,000.00 times 12 months equals $144,000.00. The excess over $117,950.00 is $26,050.00. $26,050.00 divided by $2,500.00 equals 10.42. The 10.42 amount is rounded up to 11. The reduction percentage is 22% (11 x 2% = 22%). The $2,550.00 deduction for one personal exemption is reduced by $561.00 ($2,550.00 x 22% = $561.00) to $1,989.00 ($2,550.00 - $561.00 = $1,989.00).

***   For annual gross wages above $62,700.00, this amount represents a monthly average of the Old-Age, Survivors and Disability Insurance tax based on the 1996 maximum Old-Age, Survivors and Disability Insurance tax of $3,887.40 per person (6.2% of the first $62,700.00 of annual gross wages equals $3,887.40). One-twelfth (1/2) of $3,887.40 equals $323.95.

SELF-EMPLOYED PERSONS
1996 TAX CHART
Social Security Taxes

Monthly Gross Wages	Old-Age Survivors and Disability Insurance Taxes (6.2%)*	Hospital(Medicare) Insurance Taxes (1.45%)*	Federal Income Taxes**	Net Monthly Income
100.00	11.45	2.68	-0-	85.87
200.00	22.90	5.36	-0-	171.47
300.00	34.35	8.03	-0-	257.62
400.00	45.81	10.71	-0-	343.48
500.00	57.26	13.39	-0-	429.35
600.00	68.71	16.07	1.77	513.45
700.00	80.16	18.75	15.71	585.38
800.00	91.61	21.43	29.65	657.31
900.00	103.06	24.10	43.59	729.25
1,000.00	114.51	26.78	57.53	801.18
1,100.00	125.97	29.46	71.47	873.10
1,200.00	137.42	32.14	85.41	945.03
1,300.00	148.87	34.82	99.35	1,016.96
1,400.00	160.32	37.49	113.29	1,088.90
1,500.00	171.77	40.17	127.23	1,160.83
1,600.00	183.22	42.85	141.17	1,232.76
1,700.00	194.67	45.53	155.11	1,304.69
1,800.00	206.13	48.21	169.05	1,376.61
1,900.00	217.58	50.88	182.99	1,448.55
2,000.00	229.03	53.56	196.93	1,520.48
2,100.00	240.48	56.24	210.87	1,592.41
2,200.00	251.93	58.92	224.81	1,664.34
2,300.00	263.38	61.60	238.75	1,736.27
2,400.00	274.83	64.28	252.69	1,808.20
2,500.00	286.29	66.95	266.63	1,880.13
2,600.00	297.74	69.63	280.57	1,952.06
2,700.00	309.19	72.31	294.51	1,023.99
2,800.00	320.64	74.99	315.78	2,088.59
2,900.00	332.09	77.67	341.80	2,148.44
3,000.00	343.54	80.34	367.82	2,208.30
3,100.00	354.99	83.02	393.84	2,268.15
3,200.00	366.44	85.70	419.87	2,327.99
3,300.00	377.90	88.38	445.89	2,387.83

Monthly Gross Wages	Old-Age Survivors and Disability Insurance Taxes (6.2%)*	Hospital(Medicare) Insurance Taxes (1.45%)*	Federal Income Taxes**	Net Monthly Income
3,400.00	389.35	91.06	471.91	2,447.68
3,500.00	400.80	93.74	497.93	2,507.53
3,600.00	412.25	96.41	523.95	2,567.39
3,700.00	423.70	99.09	549.98	2,627.23
3,800.00	435.15	101.77	576.00	2,687.08
3,900.00	446.60	104.55	602.02	2,746.93
4,000.00	458.06	107.13	628.04	2,806.77
4,250.00	486.68	113.82	693.10	2,956.40
4,500.00	515.31	120.52	758.15	3,106.02
4,750.00	543.94	127.21	823.31	3,255.64
5,000.00	572.57	133.91	888.26	3,405.26
5,250.00	601.20	140.60	953.31	3,554.89
5,500.00	629.83	147.30	1,018.37	3,704.50
5,750.00	647.90****	153.99	1,084.90	3,863.21
6,000.00	647.90	160.69	1,160.09	4,031.32
6,250.00	647.90	167.38	1,236.55	4,198.17
6,500.00	647.90	174.08	1,313.01	4,365.01
6,750.00	647.90	180.78	1,389.47	4,531.85
7,000.00	647.90	187.47	1,465.93	4,698.70
7,500.00	647.90	200.86	1,618.86	5,032.38
8,000.00	647.90	214.25	1,771.78	5,366.07
8,500.00	647.90	227.64	1,924.71	5,699.75
9,000.00	647.90	241.03	2,077.63	6,033.44
9,500.00	647.90	254.42	2,230.56	6,367.12
10,000.00	647.90	267.82	2,383.48	6,700.80
10,500.00	647.90	281.21	2,537.72	7,033.17
11,000.00	647.90	294.60	2,694.60	7,362.90
11,500.00	647.90	307.99	2,869.83	7,674.28
12,000.00	647.90	321.38	3,052.01	7,978.71
12,500.00	647.90	334.77	3,232.66	8,248.67
13,000.00	647.90	348.16	3,413.31	8,590.63

Footnotes to Self-Employed Persons 1996 Tax Chart:

*   Determined without regard to Section 1402(a)(12) of the Internal Revenue Code of 1986, as amended (26 U.S.C.) (the "Code").

**   In calculating each of the Old-Age, Survivors and Disability Insurance tax and the Hospital (Medicare) Insurance tax, net earning from self-employment are reduced by the deduction under Section 1402(a)(12) of the Code. The deduction under Section 1402(a)(12) of the Code is equal to net earning from self-employment (determined without regard to Section 1402(a)(12) of the Code) multiplied by one-half (1/2) of the sum of the Old-Age, Survivors and Disability Insurance tax rate (12.4%) and the Hospital (Medicare) Insurance tax rate (2.9%). The sum of these rates is 15.3% (12.4% + 2.9% = 15.3%). One-half (1/2) of the combined rate is 7.65% (15.3% x 1/2 = 7.65%).

The deduction can be computed by multiplying the net earnings from self-employment (determined without regard to Section 1402(a)(12) of the Code) by 92.35%. This gives the same deduction as multiplying the net earnings from self-employment (determined without regard to Section 1402 (a)(12) of the Code) by 7.65% and then subtracting the result.

For example, the Social Security taxes imposed on monthly net earnings form self-employment (determined with out regard to Section 1402(a)(12) of the Code) of $2,500.00 are calculated as follows:
(i) <u>Old-Age, Survivors and Disability Insurance Taxes</u>:
        $2,500.00 x 92.35% x 12.4% = $286.29
(ii) <u>Hospital (Medicare) Insurance Taxes</u>:
        $2,500.00 x 92.35% x 2.9% = $66.95

***   These amounts represent one-twelfth (1/12) of the annual Federal income tax calculated for a single taxpayer claiming one personal exemption ($2,550.00, subject to reduction in certain cases, as described below in this footnote) and taking the standard deduction ($4,000.00).

In calculating the annual Federal income tax, gross income is reduced by the deduction under Section 164(f) of the Code. The deduction under Section 164(f) of the Code is equal to one-half (1/2) of the self-employment taxes imposed by Section 1401 of the Code for the taxable year. For example, monthly net earnings from self-employment of $12,000.00 times 12 months equals $144,000.00. The Old-Age, Survivors and Disability Insurance taxes imposed by Section 1401 of the Code for the taxable year equal $7,774.80 ($62,700.00 x 12.4% = $7,774.80). The Hospital (Medicare) Insurance taxes imposed by Section 1401 of the Code for the taxable year equal $3,856.54 ($144,000.00 x .9235 x 2.9% =$3,856.54). The sum of the taxes imposed buy Section 1401 of the Code for the taxable year equals $11,631.34 ($7,774.80 + $3,856.54 = $11,631.34). The deduction under Section 164(f) of the Code is equal to one-half (1/2) of $11,631.34 or $5,815.67.

For a single taxpayer with an adjusted gross income in excess of $117,950.00, the deduction for the personal exemption is reduced by two percent (2%) for each $2,500.00 or fraction thereof by which adjusted gross income exceeds $117,950.00. The reduction is completed (i.e., the deduction of the personal exemption is eliminated) for adjusted gross income in excess of $240,450.00. In no case is the deduction for the personal exemption reduced by more than 100%. For example, monthly net earnings from self-employment of $12,000.00 times 12 months equals $144,000.00. The $144,000.00 amount is reduced by $5,815.67 (i.e., the deduction under Section 164(f) of the Code—see the immediately preceding paragraph of this footnote for the computation) to arrive at adjusted gross income of $138,184.33. The excess over $117,950.00 is $20,234.33. $20,234.33 divided by $2,500.00 equals 8.09. The 8.09 amount is rounded up to 9. The reduction percentage is 18% (9 x 2% = 18%). The $2,550.00 deduction for one personal exemption is reduced by $459.00 ($2,550.00 x 18% = $459.00) to $2,091.00 ($2,550.00 - $459.00 = $2,091.00)

****   For annual net earnings from self-employment (determined with regard to Section 1402(a)(12) of the Code) above $62,700.00, this amount represents a monthly average of the Old-Age, Survivors and Disability Insurance tax based on the 1996 maximum Old-Age, Survivors and Disability Insurance tax of $7,774.80 per person (12.4% of the first $62,700.00 of net earnings from self-employment (determined with regard to Section 1402(a)(12) of the Code) equals $7,774.80). One-twelfth (1/12) for $7,774.80 equals $647.90.

§ 154.062. Net Resources

(a) The court shall calculate net resources for the purpose of determining child support liability as provided by this section.

(b) Resources include:

(1) 100 percent of all wage and salary income and other compensation for personal services (including commissions, overtime pay, tips, and bonuses);

(2) interest, dividends, royalty income;

(3) self-employment income;

(4) net rental income (defined as rent after deducting operating expenses and mortgage payments, but not including noncash items such as depreciation); and

(5) all other income actually being received, including severance pay, retirement benefits, pensions, trust income, annuities, capital gains, social security benefits, unemployment benefits, disability and workers' compensation benefits, interest income from notes regardless of the source, gifts and prizes, spousal maintenance, and alimony.

(c) Resources do not include:

(1) return of principal or capital;

(2) accounts receivable; or

(3) benefits paid in accordance with aid to families with dependent children.

(d) The court shall deduct the following items from resources to determine the net resources available for child support:

(1) social security taxes;

(2) federal income tax based on the tax rate for a single person claiming one personal exemption and the standard deduction;

(3) state income tax;

(4) union dues; and

(5) expenses for health insurance coverage for the obligor's child.

§ 154.063. Party to Furnish Information

The court shall require a party to:

(1) furnish information sufficient to accurately identify that party's net resources and ability to pay child support; and

(2) produce copies of income tax returns for the past two years, a financial statement, and current pay stubs.

§ 154.064. Health Insurance for Child Presumptively Provided by Obligor

The guidelines for support of a child are based on the assumption that the court will order the obligor to provide health insurance coverage for the child in addition to the amount of child support calculated in accordance with those guidelines.

§ 154.065. Self-Employment Income

(a) Income from self-employment, whether positive or negative, includes benefits allocated to an individual from a business or undertaking in the form of a proprietorship, partnership, joint venture, close corporation, agency, or independent contractor, less ordinary and necessary expenses required to produce that income.

(b) In its discretion, the court may exclude from self-employment income amounts allowable under federal income tax laws as depreciation, tax credits, or any other business expenses shown by the evidence to be inappropriate in making the determination of income available for the purpose of calculating child support.

§ 154.066. Intentional Unemployment or Underemployment

If the actual income of the obligor is significantly less than what the obligor could earn because of intentional unemployment or underemployment, the court may apply the support guidelines to the earning potential of the obligor.

§ 154.067. Deemed Income

(a) When appropriate, in order to determine the net resources available for child support, the court may assign a reasonable amount of deemed income attributable to assets that do not currently produce income. The court shall also consider whether certain property that is not producing income can be liquidated without an unreasonable financial sacrifice because of cyclical or other market conditions. If there is no effective market for the property, the carrying costs of such an investment, including property taxes and note payments, shall be offset against the income attributed to the property.

(b) The court may assign a reasonable amount of deemed income to income-producing assets that a party has voluntarily transferred or on which earnings have intentionally been reduced.

§ 154.068. Wage or Salary Presumption

In the absence of evidence of the wages and salary income of a party, the court shall presume that the party has wages or salary equal to the federal minimum wage for a 40-hour week.

§ 154.069. Net Resources of Spouse

(a) The court may not add any portion of the net resources of a spouse to the net resources of an obligor or obligee in order to calculate the amount of child support to be ordered.

(b) The court may not subtract the needs of a spouse, or of a dependent of a spouse, from the net resources of the obligor or obligee.

§ 154.070. Child Support Received by Obligor

In a situation involving multiple households due child support, child support received by an obligor shall be added to the obligor's net resources to compute the net resources before determining the child support credit or applying the percentages in the multiple household table in this chapter.

SUBCHAPTER C. CHILD SUPPORT GUIDELINES

§ 154.121.   Guidelines for the Support of a Child
The child support guidelines in this subchapter are intended to guide the court in determining an equitable amount of child support.

§ 154.123.   Additional Factors for Court to Consider
(a) The court may order periodic child support payments in an amount other than established by the guidelines if the evidence rebuts the presumption that application of the guidelines is in the best interest of the child and justifies a variance from the guidelines.

(b) In determining whether application of the guidelines would be unjust or inappropriate under the circumstances, the court shall consider evidence of all relevant factors, including:

(1) the age and needs of the child;

(2) the ability of the parents to contribute to the support of the child;

(3) any financial resources available for the support of the child;

(4) the amount of time of possession of and access to a child;

(5) the amount of the obligee's net resources, including the earning potential of the obligee if the actual income of the obligee is significantly less than what the obligee could earn because the obligee is intentionally unemployed or underemployed and including an increase or decrease in the income of the obligee or income that may be attributed to the property and assets of the obligee;

(6) child care expenses incurred by either party in order to maintain gainful employment;

(7) whether either party has the managing conservatorship or actual physical custody of another child;

(8) the amount of alimony or spousal maintenance actually and currently being paid or received by a party;

(9) the expenses for a son or daughter for education beyond secondary school;

(10) whether the obligor or obligee has an automobile, housing, or other benefits furnished by his or her employer, another person, or a business entity;

(11) the amount of other deductions from the wage or salary income and from other compensation for personal services of the parties;

(12) provisions for health care insurance and payment of uninsured medical expenses;

(13) special or extraordinary educational, health care, or other expenses of the parties or of the child;

(14) the cost of travel in order to exercise possession of and access to a child;

(15) positive or negative cash flow from any real and personal property and assets, including a business and investments;

(16) debts or debt service assumed by either party; and

(17) any other reason consistent with the best interest of the child, taking into consideration the circumstances of the parents.

§ 154.124.   Agreement Concerning Support

(a) To promote the amicable settlement of disputes between the parties to a suit, the parties may enter into a written agreement containing provisions for support of the child and for modification of the agreement, including variations from the child support guidelines provided by Subchapter C.

(b) If the court finds that the agreement is in the child's best interest, the court shall render an order in accordance with the agreement.

(c) Terms of the agreement in the order may be enforced by all remedies available for enforcement of a judgment, including contempt, but are not enforceable as contract terms unless provided by the agreement.

(d) If the court finds the agreement is not in the child's best interest, the court may request the parties to submit a revised agreement or the court may render an order for the support of the child.

§ 154.125.   Application of Guidelines to Net Resources of $6,000 or Less

(a) The guidelines for the support of a child in this section are specifically designed to apply to situations in which the obligor's monthly net resources are $6,000 or less.

(b) If the obligor's monthly net resources are $6,000 or less, the court shall presumptively apply the following schedule in rendering the child support order:

CHILD SUPPORT GUIDELINES
BASED ON THE MONTHLY NET RESOURCES OF THE OBLIGOR

1 child	20% of Obligor's Net Resources
2 children	25% of Obligor's Net Resources
3 children	30% of Obligor's Net Resources
4 children	35% of Obligor's Net Resources
5 children	40% of Obligor's Net Resources
6+ children	Not less than the amount for 5 children.

§ 154.126.   Application of Guidelines to Net Resources of More Than $6,000 Monthly

(a) If the obligor's net resources exceed $6,000 per month, the court shall presumptively apply the percentage guidelines to the first $6,000 of the obligor's net resources. Without further reference to the percentage recommended by these guidelines, the court may order additional amounts of child support as appropriate, depending on the income of the parties and the proven needs of the child.

(b) The proper calculation of a child support order that exceeds the presumptive amount established for the first $6,000 of the obligor's net resources requires that the entire amount of the presumptive award be subtracted from the proven total needs of the child. After the presumptive award is subtracted, the court shall allocate between the parties the responsibility to meet the additional needs of the child according to the circumstances of the parties. However, in no event may the obligor be required to pay more child support than the greater of the presumptive amount or the amount equal to 100 percent of the proven needs of the child.

§ 154.128.   Computing Support for Children in More Than One Household

(a) In applying the child support guidelines for an obligor who has children in more than one household, the court shall apply the percentage guidelines in this subchapter by making the following computation:

 (1) determine the amount of child support that would be ordered if all children whom the obligor has the legal duty to support lived in one household by applying the schedule in this subchapter;

 (2) compute a child support credit for the obligor's children who are not before the court by dividing the amount determined under Subdivision (1) by the total number of children whom the obligor is obligated to support and multiplying that number by the number of the obligor's children who are not before the court;

 (3) determine the adjusted net resources of the obligor by subtracting the child support credit computed under Subdivision (2) from the net resources of the obligor; and

 (4) determine the child support amount for the children before the court by applying the percentage guidelines for one household for the number of children of the obligor before the court to the obligor's adjusted net resources.

(b) For the purpose of determining a child support credit, the total number of an obligor's children includes the children before the court for the establishment or modification of a support order and any other children, including children residing with the obligor, whom the obligor has the legal duty of support.

(c) The child support credit with respect to children for whom the obligor is obligated by an order to pay support is computed, regardless of whether the obligor is delinquent in child support payments, without regard to the amount of the order.

§ 154.129.   Alternative Method of Computing Support for Children in More Than One Household

In lieu of performing the computation under the preceding section, the court may determine the child support amount for the children before the court by applying the percentages in the table below to the obligor's net resources:

MULTIPLE FAMILY ADJUSTED GUIDELINES
(% OF NET RESOURCES)
Number of children before the court

		1	2	3	4	5	6	7
Number of	0	20.00	25.00	30.00	35.00	40.00	40.00	40.00
other	1	17.50	22.50	27.38	32.20	37.33	27.71	38.00
children for	2	16.00	20.63	25.20	30.33	35.43	36.00	36.44
whom the	3	14.75	19.00	24.00	29.00	34.00	34.67	35.20
obligor	4	13.60	18.33	23.14	28.00	32.89	33.60	34.18
has a	5	13.33	17.86	22.50	27.22	32.00	32.73	33.33
duty of	6	13.14	17.50	22.00	26.60	31.27	32.00	32.62
support	7	13.00	17.22	21.60	26.09	30.67	31.38	32.00

§ 154.130. Findings in Child Support Order

(a) Without regard to Rules 296 through 299, Texas Rules of Civil Procedure, in rendering an order of child support, the court shall make the findings required by Subsection (b) if:

(1) a party files a written request with the court not later than 10 days after the date of the hearing;

(2) a party makes an oral request in open court during the hearing; or

(3) the amount of child support ordered by the court varies from the amount computed by applying the percentage guidelines.

(b) If findings are required by this section, the court shall state whether the application of the guidelines would be unjust or inappropriate and shall state the following in the child support order:

"(1) the monthly net resources of the obligor per month are $_____;

"(2) the monthly net resources of the obligee per month are $_____;

"(3) the percentage applied to the obligor's net resources for child support by the actual order rendered by the court is _____%;

"(4) the amount of child support if the percentage guidelines are applied to the first $6,000 of the obligor's net resources is $_____;

"(5) if applicable, the specific reasons that the amount of child support per month ordered by the court varies from the amount stated in Subdivision (4) are: _____; and

"(6) if applicable, the obligor is obligated to support children in more than one household; and:

(A) the number of children before the court is _____;

(B) the number of children not before the court residing in the same household with the obligor is _____; and

(C) the number of children not before the court for whom the obligor is obligated by a court order to pay support, without regard to whether the obligor is delinquent in child support payments, and who are not counted under Paragraph (A) or (B) is _____."

§ 154.181. Medical Support Order

In a suit affecting the parent-child relationship or in a proceeding under Chapter 159, the court shall render an order for the medical support of the child.

§ 154.182. Health Insurance

(a) The court shall consider the cost and quality of health insurance coverage available to the parties and shall give priority to health insurance coverage available through the employment of one of the parties.

(b) In determining the manner in which health insurance for the child is to be ordered, the court shall render its order in accordance with the following priorities, unless a party shows good cause why a particular order would not be in the best interest of the child:

(1) if health insurance is available for the child through the obligor's employment or membership in a union, trade association, or other organization, the court shall order the obligor to include the child in the obligor's health insurance;

(2) if health insurance is not available for the child through the obligor's employment but is available for the child through obligee's employment or membership in a union, trade association, or other organization, the court may order the obligee to provide health insurance for the child, and, in such event, shall order the obligor to pay additional child support to be withheld from earnings under Chapter 158 to the obligee for the actual cost of the health insurance for the child; or

(3) if health insurance is not available for the child under Subdivision (1) of (2), the court shall order the obligor to provide health insurance for the child if the court finds that health insurance is available for the child from another source and that the obligor is financially able to provide it.

§ 154.183. Health Insurance Additional Support Duty of Obligor

(a) An amount that an obligor is required to pay for health insurance for the child:

(1) is in addition to the amount that the obligor is required to pay for child support under the guidelines for child support;

(2) is a child support obligation; and

(3) may be enforced as a child support obligation.

(b) If the court finds and states in the child support order that the obligee will maintain health insurance coverage for the child at the obligee's expense, the court may increase the amount of child support to be paid by the obligor in an amount not exceeding the total expense to the obligee for maintaining health insurance coverage.

(c) As additional child support, the court shall allocate between the parties, according to their circumstances, the reasonable and necessary health care expenses of a child that are not reimbursed by health insurance.

§ 154.184. Effect of Order

(a) Receipt of a medical support order requiring that health insurance be provided for a child shall be considered a change in the family circumstances of the employee or member, for health insurance purposes, equivalent to the birth or adoption of a child.

(b) The child shall be automatically enrolled for the first 31 days after the receipt of the order by the employer on the same terms and conditions as apply to any other dependent child.

(c) The employer shall notify the insurer of the automatic enrollment.

(d) During the 31-day period, the employer and insurer shall complete all necessary forms and procedures to make the enrollment permanent or shall report in accordance with this subchapter the reasons the coverage cannot be made permanent.

Appendix B
Forms

The following is a list of the forms found in this appendix. Each form is numbered in the upper outside corner. Be sure you have the correct form number because several of the forms have the same title and appear very similar. The page number where the form begins is also listed below.

Table of Forms

WHERE TO FIND ADDITIONAL FORMS. This book is designed for the most typical divorce situations. In unusual situations there are numerous other forms that can be filed to obtain various results. To find additional forms, check your nearest law library. Ask the librarian where to find divorce form books. There are specific guides to divorce matters that will contain forms, and there are also general form books containing forms on all kinds of legal matters. (Also see the section on LEGAL RESEARCH in chapter 2.)

(1) S	(2) DESCRIPTION	(3) ID#	(4) VALUE	(5) BALANCE OWED	(6) EQUITY	(7) OWNER H-W-J	(8) H	(9) W

form 2

(1) S	(2) CREDITOR	(3) ACCOUNT NO.	(4) NOTES	(5) MONTHLY PAYMENT	(6) BALANCE OWED	(7) DATE	(8) OWNER H-W-J	(9) H	(10) W

CHILD SUPPORT GUIDELINES WORKSHEET

		Father	Mother
		Father	Mother
Step 1:	Determine monthly gross income: (Schedule A)	$	$
Step 2:	Determine monthly deductions: (Schedule B)	$	$
Step 3:	Determine Monthly Net Resources (Subtract Step 2 from Step 1)	$	$
Step 4:	Determine child support guideline amount (Schedule C)	$	$

SCHEDULE A

AVERAGE <u>GROSS MONTHLY</u> income shall include the following:

		FATHER per month	MOTHER per month
a.	Gross Salary or Wages (AFDC excluded)		
b.	Bonuses, Commissions, Allowance, Overtime, tips, etc.		
c.	Business Income from sources such as self-employment, partnership, close corporations, joint ventures, and/or independent contractors (gross receipts minus ordinary and necessary expenses required to produce income)		
d.	Disability Benefits		
e.	Workers' Compensation		
f.	Unemployment Compensation		
g.	Pension, Retirement, or Annuity payments		
h.	Social Security Benefits		
i.	Spousal Support received from prior marriage		
j.	Interest, Dividends, Royalty Income		
k.	Income from trusts and estates		
l.	Rental Income (gross receipts minus ordinary and necessary expenses required to produce income)		
m.	Gains derived from dealing in property (not including nonrecurring gains)		
n.	Itemize any other income of a recurring nature or factor considered		
TOTAL MONTHLY GROSS INCOME:		$	$

SCHEDULE B

THE JUDGE SHALL DEDUCT THE FOLLOWING FROM GROSS INCOME

		FATHER per month	MOTHER per month
a.	Federal income taxes (based on withholding for a single person claiming one personal exemption and the standard deduction)		
b.	F.I.C.A or self-employment taxes		
c.	Mandatory union dues		
d.	Health insurance payments for the child		
	TOTAL ALLOWABLE MONTHLY DEDUCTIONS	$	$

SCHEDULE C

Child Support Based On
Monthly Net Resources Of The Obligor

1 child   20% of Obligor's Net Resources

2 children   25% of Obligor's Net Resources

3 children   30% of Obligor's Net Resources

4 children   35% of Obligor's Net Resources

5 children   40% of Obligor's Net Resources

6+ children   Not less than the amount for 5 children

Note: If the Obligor's net resources exceed $6,000 per month, the percentages set forth above are applied to the first $6,000. The court may order additional support depending upon the needs of the child.

SCHEDULE   D

Other Factors To Be Considered
In Determining Child Support

The court may take into account the following factors when determining child support and may adjust the amount determined under the guidelines accordingly:

1. The amount of net resources the obligor could have if he is intentionally unemployed or underemployed to avoid payment of child support.

2. Age and needs of the child.

3. Child care expenses incurred by either parent to maintain employment.

4. Whether the parent has physical custody of another child.

5. The amount of child support being paid or received by either parent under another child support order.

6. Education expenses for a child beyond high school.

7. Other resources provided by an employer, business or other person (automobile, housing, etc.)

8. Alimony or spousal support being paid or received.

9. Amount of other deductions from wages.

10. Provision for health care insurance and payment of uninsured medical expenses.

11. Spousal or extraordinary educational, health care, or other expenses of the parents or child.

12. Cost of travel to visit the child.

13. Positive or negative cash flow from any real and personal property and assets.

14. Debts assumed by either parent.

15. Any other reason consistent with the best interest of the child taking into consideration the circumstances of the parents.

NO. _____

IN THE MATTER OF	§	IN THE DISTRICT COURT
THE MARRIAGE OF	§	
	§	
_____	§	_____ JUDICIAL DISTRICT
	§	
AND	§	
	§	
_____	§	_____ COUNTY, TEXAS

ORIGINAL PETITION FOR DIVORCE

TO THE HONORABLE JUDGE OF SAID COURT:

This suit is brought by _____, Petitioner, social security number _____, who is ____ years of age and resides in _____ County, Texas. Respondent,_____ _____, social security number _____, is ____ years of age and resides at _____.

I.
Petitioner has been a domiciliary of the State of Texas for the preceding six-month period and a resident of _____ County for the preceding ninety-day period.

II.
No process is necessary at this time.

III.
The parties were married on or about _____, _____, in _____, [and ceased to live together as husband and wife on or about _____, _____].

The marriage has become insupportable because of discord or conflict of personalities between Petitioner and Respondent that destroys the legitimate ends of the marriage relationship and prevents any reasonable expectation of reconciliation.

IV.
There are no minor or dependent children born or adopted of this marriage and none is expected.

V.

Petitioner requests the Court to order a division of the estate of the Parties in a manner that the Court deems just and right, as provided by law.

VI.

Petitioner requests a change of name to _____.

VII.

A protective order under Chapter 71 or Section 3.581 of the Texas Family Code is/is not in effect with regard to the parties of this suit.

(The protective order was issued by the _____ Court in Cause No. _____ and was entered on the following date: _____. A copy of the protective order is attached to this petition.)

WHEREFORE Petitioner prays that citation and notice issue as required by law and that the Court grant a divorce and decree such other relief as more specifically requested in this Petition.

Petitioner prays that Petitioner's name be changed as requested above.

Petitioner prays that Respondent be ordered to pay the fees and costs of this suit.

Petitioner prays for general relief.

Respectfully submitted,

_____

Name: _____

Address: _____

_____

Telephone: _____

I AM AWARE THAT IT IS THE POLICY OF THE STATE OF TEXAS TO PROMOTE THE AMICABLE AND NONJUDICIAL SETTLEMENT OF DISPUTES INVOLVING CHILDREN AND FAMILIES. I AM AWARE OF ALTERNATIVE DISPUTE RESOLUTION METHODS, INCLUDING MEDIATION. WHILE I RECOGNIZE THAT ALTERNATIVE DISPUTE RESOLUTION IS AN ALTERNATIVE TO AND NOT A SUBSTITUTE FOR A TRIAL AND THAT THIS CASE MAY BE TRIED IF IT IS NOT SETTLED, I REPRESENT TO THE COURT THAT I WILL ATTEMPT IN GOOD FAITH TO RESOLVE CONTESTED ISSUES IN THIS CASE BY ALTERNATIVE DISPUTE RESOLUTION WITHOUT THE NECESSITY OF COURT INTERVENTION.

_____

Name

NO. _____

IN THE MATTER OF THE MARRIAGE OF	§ § §	IN THE DISTRICT COURT

_____ § _____ JUDICIAL DISTRICT

AND § §

_____ § _____ COUNTY, TEXAS

ORIGINAL PETITION FOR DIVORCE

TO THE HONORABLE JUDGE OF SAID COURT:

    This suit is brought by _____, Petitioner, social security number _____, who is ____ years of age and resides in _____ County, Texas. Respondent,_____ _____, social security number _____, is ____ years of age and resides at _____.

I.
    Petitioner has been a domiciliary of the State of Texas for the preceding six-month period and a resident of _____ County for the preceding ninety-day period.

II.
    Process should be served on Respondent at _____ _____.

III.
    The parties were married on or about _____, _____, in _____, [and ceased to live together as husband and wife on or about _____, _____].

    The marriage has become insupportable because of discord or conflict of personalities between Petitioner and Respondent that destroys the legitimate ends of the marriage relationship and prevents any reasonable expectation of reconciliation.

IV.
    There are no minor or dependent children born or adopted of this marriage and none is expected.

V.

Petitioner requests the Court to order a division of the estate of the Parties in a manner that the Court deems just and right, as provided by law.

VI.

Petitioner requests a change of name to _____.

VII.

A protective order under Chapter 71 or Section 3.581 of the Texas Family Code is/is not in effect with regard to the parties of this suit.

(The protective order was issued by the _____ Court in Cause No. _____ and was entered on the following date: _____. A copy of the protective order is attached to this petition.)

WHEREFORE Petitioner prays that citation and notice issue as required by law and that the Court grant a divorce and decree such other relief as more specifically requested in this Petition.

Petitioner prays that Petitioner's name be changed as requested above.

Petitioner prays that Respondent be ordered to pay the fees and costs of this suit.

Petitioner prays for general relief.

Respectfully submitted,

_____

Name: _____

Address: _____

_____

Telephone: _____

I AM AWARE THAT IT IS THE POLICY OF THE STATE OF TEXAS TO PROMOTE THE AMICABLE AND NONJUDICIAL SETTLEMENT OF DISPUTES INVOLVING CHILDREN AND FAMILIES. I AM AWARE OF ALTERNATIVE DISPUTE RESOLUTION METHODS, INCLUDING MEDIATION. WHILE I RECOGNIZE THAT ALTERNATIVE DISPUTE RESOLUTION IS AN ALTERNATIVE TO AND NOT A SUBSTITUTE FOR A TRIAL AND THAT THIS CASE MAY BE TRIED IF IT IS NOT SETTLED, I REPRESENT TO THE COURT THAT I WILL ATTEMPT IN GOOD FAITH TO RESOLVE CONTESTED ISSUES IN THIS CASE BY ALTERNATIVE DISPUTE RESOLUTION WITHOUT THE NECESSITY OF COURT INTERVENTION.

_____

Name

NO. _____

IN THE MATTER OF THE MARRIAGE OF	§	IN THE DISTRICT COURT
	§	
	§	
_____	§	_____ JUDICIAL DISTRICT
	§	
AND	§	
	§	
	§	
_____	§	_____ COUNTY, TEXAS

ORIGINAL PETITION FOR DIVORCE

TO THE HONORABLE JUDGE OF SAID COURT:

This suit is brought by _____, Petitioner, social security number _____, who is ____ years of age and resides in _____ County, Texas. Respondent,_____ _____, social security number _____, is ____ years of age. Respondent's place of residence is unknown.

I.
Petitioner has been a domiciliary of the State of Texas for the preceding six-month period and a resident of _____ County for the preceding ninety-day period.

II.
Citation by publication or other substituted service is necessary for the reasons set forth in the attached affidavit.

III.
The parties were married on or about _____, _____, in _____, [and ceased to live together as husband and wife on or about _____, _____].

The marriage has become insupportable because of discord or conflict of personalities between Petitioner and Respondent that destroys the legitimate ends of the marriage relationship and prevents any reasonable expectation of reconciliation.

IV.
There are no minor or dependent children born or adopted of this marriage and none is expected.

NO. _____

IN THE MATTER OF THE MARRIAGE OF	§	IN THE DISTRICT COURT

_____ §

AND §

_____ § _____ JUDICIAL DISTRICT

AND IN THE INTERESTS OF §

_____ §

_____, and §

_____ §

MINOR CHILDREN § _____ COUNTY, TEXAS

AFFIDAVIT OF INABILITY TO PAY COURT COSTS

BEFORE ME, the undersigned authority, on this day personally appeared _____ who, after being by me duly sworn stated under oath as follows:

1. My total monthly income is $_____.

2. I receive employment income of $_____.
    My employer's name is: _____.
    My employer's address is: _____
    _____.

3. I receive additional monthly income of $ _____.
    The source of this income is _____
    _____.

4. The following people are dependent upon me for support:
    <u>Name</u>   <u>Age</u>
    Self_____   _____

    _____   _____

    _____   _____

5. I DO/DO NOT have a checking account.
    Checking account balance $_____

6.　　I DO/DO NOT have a savings account.
　　　Savings account balance $_____

7.　　I own the following property (e.g. real estate, stocks, bonds, notes, automobiles)
　　　excluding ordinary household furnishings and clothing:

Property	Value	Encumbrance
_____	_____	_____
_____	_____	_____
_____	_____	_____
_____	_____	_____

8.　　I have the following monthly expenses:

　　　　　　　　　　　　　　　　　　　　　　　　Amount

a. Rent/Mortgage　　　　　　　　　　　　　_____
b. Food　　　　　　　　　　　　　　　　　_____
c. Clothing　　　　　　　　　　　　　　　_____
d. Transportation　　　　　　　　　　　　_____
e. Utilities　　　　　　　　　　　　　　　_____
f. Child Care　　　　　　　　　　　　　　_____
g. _____　　　　　　　　_____
h. _____　　　　　　　　_____

I am unable to pay the court costs.

I verify that the statements made in this affidavit are true and correct.

　　　　　　　　　　　　　　　　　　_____
　　　　　　　　　　　　　　　　　　AFFIANT

SUBSCRIBED AND SWORN to before me on this _____ day of_____,
_____.

_____
Notary Public State of Texas
My Commission Expires:

_____

NO. _____

IN THE MATTER OF	§	IN THE DISTRICT COURT
THE MARRIAGE OF	§	
	§	
_____	§	
	§	
AND	§	
	§	
_____	§	_____ JUDICIAL DISTRICT
	§	
AND IN THE INTERESTS OF	§	
	§	
_____	§	
	§	
_____, and	§	
	§	
_____	§	
MINOR CHILDREN	§	_____ COUNTY, TEXAS

TEMPORARY ORDERS

On the _____ day of _____, _____, came on to be heard the application of _____ for temporary orders.

Petitioner, _____, appeared in person.

Respondent, _____, appeared in person.

[Respondent, _____, although duly and properly notified, did not appear.]

The Court, having considered the pleadings and heard the evidence, finds that all necessary prerequisites of the law have been legally satisfied and that this Court has jurisdiction over the parties and subject matter of this cause.

The Court finds that the following orders for the safety and welfare of the children are in the best interest of the children.

IT IS ORDERED that _____ be and is hereby appointed Temporary Managing Conservator of the following children:

_____

_____.

IT IS ORDERED that _____ be and is hereby appointed Temporary Possessory Conservator of the following children: _____
_____.

IT IS ORDERED that the Temporary Possessory Conservator shall have possession of the children in accordance with the Standard Possession Order, attached as Exhibit "A", which is incorporated for all purposes.

IT IS ORDERED that _____ as temporary sole managing conservator and _____ as temporary possessory conservator at all time shall each retain the following rights and duties:

(1) To receive information from the other parent concerning the health, education, and welfare of the children;

(2) To inform the other parent in a timely manner of significant information concerning the health, education, and welfare of the children;

(3) To confer with the other parent to the extent possible before making a decision concerning the health, education, and welfare of the children;

(4) To have access to medical, dental, psychological, and educational records of the children;

(5) To consult with any physician, dentist, or psychologist of the children;

(6) To consult with school officials concerning the children's welfare and educational status, including school activities;

(7) To attend school activities;

(8) To be designated on any records as a person to be notified in case of an emergency;

(9) To consent to medical, dental, and surgical treatment during an emergency involving an immediate danger to the health and safety of the children; and

(10) To manage the estate of the children to the extent the estate has been created by the parent or the parent's family.

IT IS ORDERED that _____ and _____ shall each retain the following rights and duties during their respective periods of possession:

(1) The duty of care, control, protection, and reasonable discipline of the children;

(2) The duty to support the children, including providing the children with food, clothing, and shelter, and medical and dental care not involving an invasive procedure;

(3) The right to consent to medical and surgical treatment of the children not involving an invasive procedure; and

(4) The right to direct the moral and religious training of the children.

IT IS ORDERED that _____ as temporary sole managing conservator exclusively has the following rights, privileges, duties, and powers:

(1) The right to establish the primary residence of the children;

(2) The right to consent to medical, dental, and surgical treatment involving invasive procedures, and to consent to psychiatric and psychological treatment of the children;

(3) The right to receive and give receipt for payments for the support of the children and to hold or disburse any funds for the benefit of the children;

(4) The right to represent the children in legal proceedings and to make other decisions of substantial legal significance concerning the children;

(5) The right to consent to marriage and to enlistment in the armed forces of the United States;

(6) The right to make decisions concerning the children's education;

(7) The right to the services and earnings of the children; and

(8) Except when a guardian of the children's estates or a guardian or attorney ad litem has been appointed for the children, the right to act as an agent of the children in relation to the children's estates if the children's estates is required by the state, the United States, or a foreign government.

IT IS ORDERED that _____ pay to
_____ for the support of
_____
_____ $_____ per _____, with the first installment being due and payable on _____, _____, and a like installment being due and payable on each _____ and _____ day of each and every _____ thereafter until further order of this Court.

IT IS ORDERED that _____ make all said payments through the _____ County Child Support Office, _____, Texas.

IT IS ORDERED that _____ pay to _____ as temporary support $_____ per _____, with the first installment being due and payable on _____, _____, and a like installment being due and payable on each _____ and _____ day of each and every _____ thereafter until further order of this Court.

IT IS ORDERED that _____ make all said payments through the _____ County Child Support Office, _____, _____, Texas.

The Court finds that the following orders respecting the property and parties are necessary and equitable.

IT IS ORDERED that _____ have the exclusive use and possession of the following property during the pendency of this suit:

1. All furniture, furnishings and fixtures currently in _____ _____'s possession.

2. The _____ motor vehicle.

3. All clothing, jewelry and personal effects currently in _____ _____'s possession.

4. The residence located at _____.

5. _____.

IT IS ORDERED that _____ have the exclusive use and possession of the following property during the pendency of this suit:

1. All furniture, furnishings and fixtures currently in _____ _____'s possession.

2. The _____ motor vehicle.

3. All clothing, jewelry and personal effects currently in _____ _____'s possession.

4. The residence located at _____.

5. _____.

IT IS ORDERED that _____ shall pay the following debts, liabilities and obligations during the pendency of this case:

1. All ordinary and necessary living expenses incurred by _____ _____ or the parties' minor children except as may be specifically set forth hereinabove.

2. The monthly mortgage payment together with all utilities and maintenance for the residence located at_____ _____.

3. The monthly debts due and payable on the _____ _____ motor vehicle.

4. _____.

5. _____.

IT IS ORDERED that _____ shall pay the following debts, liabilities and obligations during the pendency of this case:

1. All ordinary and necessary living expenses incurred by _____ _____.

2. The monthly debts due and payable on the _____ _____ motor vehicle.

3. _____.

4. _____.

IT IS ORDERED that _____ shall maintain in full force and effect the medical and health insurance coverage on the children and Petitioner and Respondent shall each be responsible for one-half ($^1/_2$) of all medical expenses of the children not covered by insurance.

IT IS ORDERED that both parties file with each other and the Clerk of this Court a sworn inventory and appraisement of all the separate and community property owned by the parties and of all debts owed by the parties, said inventory to be filed forty-five (45) days after the entry by the Court of these Agreed Temporary Orders.

IT IS ORDERED that this case is set for trial on the merits on the _____ day of _____, _____, at _____ o'clock ___.m.

All said temporary orders are without prejudice to either party to petition the Court for new or additional orders.

All said temporary orders shall continue in full force and effect until further order of this Court.

SIGNED this _____ day of _____, _____.

_____

Judge Presiding

NO. _____

IN THE MATTER OF   §   IN THE DISTRICT COURT
THE MARRIAGE OF   §
     §
_____ §   _____ JUDICIAL DISTRICT
     §
AND   §
     §
_____ §   _____ COUNTY, TEXAS

TEMPORARY ORDERS

On the _____ day of_____, _____, came on to be heard the application of _____ for temporary orders.

Petitioner, _____, appeared in person and announced ready.

Respondent, _____, appeared in person and announced ready.

[Respondent, _____, although duly and properly notified, did not appear.]

The Court, having considered the pleadings and heard the evidence and argument of the parties or their counsel, finds that all necessary prerequisites of the law have been legally satisfied and that this Court has jurisdiction over the parties and subject matter of this cause.

The Court finds that there are no children of this marriage under 18 years of age or otherwise entitled to support.

The Court finds that the following orders respecting the property and parties are necessary and equitable.

IT IS ORDERED that _____ pay to _____ as temporary support $_____ per _____, with the first installment being due and payable on _____, _____, and a like installment being due and payable on each _____ and _____ day of each and every month thereafter until further order of this Court.

IT IS ORDERED that _____ make all said payments through the _____ County Child Support Office, _____, Texas.

IT IS ORDERED that _____ have the exclusive use and possession of the following property during the pendency of this suit:

1. All furniture, furnishings and fixtures currently in _____ _____'s possession.

2. The _____ motor vehicle.

3. All clothing, jewelry and personal effects currently in _____ _____'s possession.

4. The residence located at _____.

5. _____.

IT IS ORDERED that _____ have the exclusive use and possession of the following property during the pendency of this suit:

1. All furniture, furnishings and fixtures currently in _____ _____'s possession.

2. The _____ motor vehicle.

3. All clothing, jewelry and personal effects currently in _____ _____'s possession.

4. The residence located at _____.

5. _____.

IT IS ORDERED that _____ shall pay the following debts, liabilities and obligations during the pendency of this case:

1. All ordinary and necessary living expenses incurred by _____.

2. The monthly mortgage payment together with all utilities and maintenance for the residence located at_____ _____.

3. The monthly debts due and payable on the _____ motor vehicle.
4. _____.

5. _____.

INDEX

Your #1 Source for Real World Legal Information...

SPHINX® PUBLISHING

A Division of Sourcebooks, Inc.®

- Written by lawyers
- Simple English explanation of the law
- Forms and instructions included

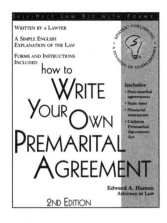 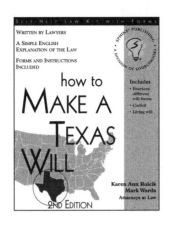 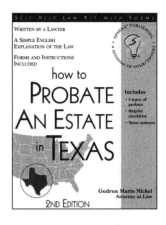

HOW TO WRITE YOUR OWN PREMARITAL AGREEMENT

With a divorce rate of over 50 percent, it is wise to consider drafting your own premarital agreement. With this book, you can also cancel or modify an existing premarital agreement. Includes state-by-state summary of inheritance and divorce laws, with forms and instructions.

192 pages; $21.95;
ISBN 1-57071-344-8

HOW TO MAKE A TEXAS WILL, 2ND ED.

This book includes ready-to-use forms and instructions that take care of the many issues, such as Texas inheritance laws and joint property, that affect a will in Texas.

112 pages; $16.95;
ISBN 1-57248-417-7

HOW TO PROBATE AN ESTATE IN TEXAS, 2ND ED.

An easy-to-use handbook explaining the process of probate in Texas. Saves time, money, and frustration. Includes forms and instructions.

208 pages; $22.95;
ISBN 1-57071-418-5

See the following order form for books written specifically for California, Florida, Georgia, Illinois, Massachusetts, Michigan, Minnesota, New York, North Carolina, Ohio, Pennsylvania, and Texas!

What our customers say about our books:

"It couldn't be more clear for the lay person." —R.D.

"I want you to know I really appreciate your book. It has saved me a lot of time and money." —L.T.

"Your real estate contracts book has saved me nearly $12,000.00 in closing costs over the past year." —A.B.

"...many of the legal questions that I have had over the years were answered clearly and concisely through your plain English interpretation of the law." —C.E.H.

"If there weren't people out there like you I'd be lost. You have the best books of this type out there." —S.B.

"...your forms and directions are easy to follow." —C.V.M.

Sphinx Publishing's Legal Survival Guides
are directly available from the Sourcebooks, Inc., or from your local bookstores.

For credit card orders call 1–800–432–7444, write P.O. Box 4410, Naperville, IL 60567-4410,
or fax 630-961-2168

SPHINX® PUBLISHING'S NATIONAL TITLES
Valid in All 50 States

LEGAL SURVIVAL IN BUSINESS

How to Form a Delaware Corporation from Any State	$24.95
How to Form a Limited Liability Company	$22.95
How to Form a Nevada Corporation from Any State	$24.95
How to Form a Nonprofit Corporation	$24.95
How to Form Your Own Corporation (3E)	$24.95
How to Form Your Own Partnership	$22.95
How to Register Your Own Copyright (3E)	$21.95
How to Register Your Own Trademark (3E)	$21.95
Most Valuable Business Legal Forms You'll Ever Need (2E)	$19.95
Most Valuable Corporate Forms You'll Ever Need (2E)	$24.95

LEGAL SURVIVAL IN COURT

Debtors' Rights (3E)	$14.95
Grandparents' Rights (3E)	$24.95
Help Your Lawyer Win Your Case (2E)	$14.95
Jurors' Rights (2E)	$12.95
Legal Research Made Easy (2E)	$14.95
Winning Your Personal Injury Claim (2E)	$24.95

LEGAL SURVIVAL IN REAL ESTATE

How to Buy a Condominium or Townhome	$19.95
How to Negotiate Real Estate Contracts (3E)	$18.95
How to Negotiate Real Estate Leases (3E)	$18.95

LEGAL SURVIVAL IN PERSONAL AFFAIRS

Como Hacer su Propio Testamento	$16.95
Guia de Inmigracion a Estados Unidos (2E)	$24.95
Como Solicitar su Propio Divorcio	$24.95
How to File Your Own Bankruptcy (4E)	$19.95
How to File Your Own Divorce (4E)	$24.95
How to Make Your Own Will (2E)	$16.95
How to Write Your Own Living Will (2E)	$16.95
How to Write Your Own Premarital Agreement (2E)	$21.95
How to Win Your Unemployment Compensation Claim	$19.95
Living Trusts and Simple Ways to Avoid Probate (2E)	$22.95
Most Valuable Personal Legal Forms You'll Ever Need	$19.95
Neighbor v. Neighbor (2E)	$16.95
The Nanny and Domestic Help Legal Kit	$22.95
The Power of Attorney Handbook (3E)	$19.95
Social Security Benefits Handbook (2E)	$16.95
Unmarried Parents' Rights	$19.95
U.S.A. Immigration Guide (3E)	$19.95
Your Right to Child Custody, Visitation and Support	$22.95

Legal Survival Guides are directly available from Sourcebooks, Inc., or from your local bookstores.
Prices are subject to change without notice.

For credit card orders call 1–800–432–7444, write P.O. Box 4410, Naperville, IL 60567-4410
or fax 630-961-2168

SPHINX® PUBLISHING ORDER FORM

BILL TO:		SHIP TO:	
Phone #	Terms	F.O.B. Chicago, IL	Ship Date

Charge my: ☐ VISA　　☐ MasterCard　　☐ American Express

☐ **Money Order or Personal Check**

Credit Card Number　　　　　　　　　　　　　　　　Expiration Date

Qty	ISBN	Title	Retail	Ext.	Qty	ISBN	Title	Retail	Ext.
		SPHINX PUBLISHING NATIONAL TITLES				1-57071-345-6	Most Valuable Bus. Legal Forms You'll Ever Need (2E)	$19.95	
	1-57248-148-X	Como Hacer su Propio Testamento	$16.95			1-57071-346-4	Most Valuable Corporate Forms You'll Ever Need (2E)	$24.95	
	1-57248-147-1	Como Solicitar su Propio Divorcio	$24.95			1-57248-130-7	Most Valuable Personal Legal Forms You'll Ever Need	$19.95	
	1-57071-342-1	Debtors' Rights (3E)	$14.95			1-57248-098-X	The Nanny and Domestic Help Legal Kit	$22.95	
	1-57248-139-0	Grandparents' Rights (3E)	$24.95			1-57248-089-0	Neighbor v. Neighbor (2E)	$16.95	
	1-57248-087-4	Guia de Immigracion a Estados Unidos (2E)	$24.95			1-57071-348-0	The Power of Attorney Handbook (3E)	$19.95	
	1-57248-103-X	Help Your Lawyer Win Your Case (2E)	$14.95			1-57071-337-5	Social Security Benefits Handbook (2E)	$16.95	
	1-57071-164-X	How to Buy a Condominium or Townhome	$19.95			1-57071-399-5	Unmarried Parents' Rights	$19.95	
	1-57071-223-9	How to File Your Own Bankruptcy (4E)	$19.95			1-57071-354-5	U.S.A. Immigration Guide (3E)	$19.95	
	1-57248-132-3	How to File Your Own Divorce (4E)	$24.95			1-57248-138-2	Winning Your Personal Injury Claim (2E)	$24.95	
	1-57248-100-5	How to Form a DE Corporation from Any State	$24.95			1-57248-097-1	Your Right to Child Custody, Visitation and Support	$22.95	
	1-57248-083-1	How to Form a Limited Liability Company	$22.95				**CALIFORNIA TITLES**		
	1-57248-101-3	How to Form a NV Corporation from Any State	$24.95			1-57248-150-1	CA Power of Attorney Handbook (2E)	$18.95	
	1-57248-099-8	How to Form a Nonprofit Corporation	$24.95			1-57248-151-X	How to File for Divorce in CA (3E)	$26.95	
	1-57248-133-1	How to Form Your Own Corporation (3E)	$24.95			1-57071-356-1	How to Make a CA Will	$16.95	
	1-57071-343-X	How to Form Your Own Partnership	$22.95			1-57248-145-5	How to Probate and Settle an Estate in California	$26.95	
	1-57248-119-6	How to Make Your Own Will (2E)	$16.95			1-57248-146-3	How to Start a Business in CA	$18.95	
	1-57071-331-6	How to Negotiate Real Estate Contracts (3E)	$18.95			1-57071-358-8	How to Win in Small Claims Court in CA	$16.95	
	1-57071-332-4	How to Negotiate Real Estate Leases (3E)	$18.95			1-57071-359-6	Landlords' Rights and Duties in CA	$21.95	
	1-57248-124-2	How to Register Your Own Copyright (3E)	$21.95				**FLORIDA TITLES**		
	1-57248-104-8	How to Register Your Own Trademark (3E)	$21.95			1-57071-363-4	Florida Power of Attorney Handbook (2E)	$16.95	
	1-57071-349-9	How to Win Your Unemployment Compensation Claim	$19.95			1-57248-093-9	How to File for Divorce in FL (6E)	$24.95	
	1-57248-118-8	How to Write Your Own Living Will (2E)	$16.95			1-57071-380-4	How to Form a Corporation in FL (4E)	$24.95	
	1-57071-344-8	How to Write Your Own Premarital Agreement (2E)	$21.95			1-57248-086-6	How to Form a Limited Liability Co. in FL	$22.95	
	1-57071-333-2	Jurors' Rights (2E)	$12.95			1-57071-401-0	How to Form a Partnership in FL	$22.95	
	1-57071-400-2	Legal Research Made Easy (2E)	$14.95			1-57248-113-7	How to Make a FL Will (6E)	$16.95	
	1-57071-336-7	Living Trusts and Simple Ways to Avoid Probate (2E)	$22.95			1-57248-088-2	How to Modify Your FL Divorce Judgment (4E)	$24.95	

Form Continued on Following Page　　　　**SUBTOTAL**

To order, call Sourcebooks at 1-800-432-7444 or FAX (630) 961-2168 (Bookstores, libraries, wholesalers—please call for discount)

Prices are subject to change without notice.

SPHINX® PUBLISHING ORDER FORM

Qty	ISBN	Title	Retail	Ext.
_____	1-57248-081-5	How to Start a Business in FL (5E)	$16.95	_____
_____	1-57071-362-6	How to Win in Small Claims Court in FL (6E)	$16.95	_____
_____	1-57248-123-4	Landlords' Rights and Duties in FL (8E)	$21.95	_____
GEORGIA TITLES				
_____	1-57248-137-4	How to File for Divorce in GA (4E)	$21.95	_____
_____	1-57248-075-0	How to Make a GA Will (3E)	$16.95	_____
_____	1-57248-140-4	How to Start a Business in Georgia (2E)	$16.95	_____
ILLINOIS TITLES				
_____	1-57071-405-3	How to File for Divorce in IL (2E)	$21.95	_____
_____	1-57071-415-0	How to Make an IL Will (2E)	$16.95	_____
_____	1-57071-416-9	How to Start a Business in IL (2E)	$16.95	_____
_____	1-57248-078-5	Landlords' Rights & Duties in IL	$21.95	_____
MASSACHUSETTS TITLES				
_____	1-57248-128-5	How to File for Divorce in MA (3E)	$24.95	_____
_____	1-57248-115-3	How to Form a Corporation in MA	$24.95	_____
_____	1-57248-108-0	How to Make a MA Will (2E)	$16.95	_____
_____	1-57248-106-4	How to Start a Business in MA (2E)	$16.95	_____
_____	1-57248-107-2	Landlords' Rights and Duties in MA (2E)	$21.95	_____
MICHIGAN TITLES				
_____	1-57071-409-6	How to File for Divorce in MI (2E)	$21.95	_____
_____	1-57248-077-7	How to Make a MI Will (2E)	$16.95	_____
_____	1-57071-407-X	How to Start a Business in MI (2E)	$16.95	_____
NEW YORK TITLES				
_____	1-57248-141-2	How to File for Divorce in NY (2E)	$26.95	_____
_____	1-57248-105-6	How to Form a Corporation in NY	$24.95	_____
_____	1-57248-095-5	How to Make a NY Will (2E)	$16.95	_____
_____	1-57071-185-2	How to Start a Business in NY	$16.95	_____
_____	1-57071-187-9	How to Win in Small Claims Court in NY	$16.95	_____
_____	1-57071-186-0	Landlords' Rights and Duties in NY	$21.95	_____
_____	1-57071-188-7	New York Power of Attorney Handbook	$19.95	_____
_____	1-57248-122-6	Tenants' Rights in NY	$21..95	_____

Qty	ISBN	Title	Retail	Ext.
NORTH CAROLINA TITLES				
_____	1-57071-326-X	How to File for Divorce in NC (2E)	$22.95	_____
_____	1-57248-129-3	How to Make a NC Will (3E)	$16.95	_____
_____	1-57248-096-3	How to Start a Business in NC (2E)	$16.95	_____
_____	1-57248-091-2	Landlords' Rights & Duties in NC	$21.95	_____
OHIO TITLES				
_____	1-57248-102-1	How to File for Divorce in OH	$24.95	_____
PENNSYLVANIA TITLES				
_____	1-57248-127-7	How to File for Divorce in PA (2E)	$24.95	_____
_____	1-57248-094-7	How to Make a PA Will (2E)	$16.95	_____
_____	1-57248-112-9	How to Start a Business in PA (2E)	$18.95	_____
_____	1-57071-179-8	Landlords' Rights and Duties in PA	$19.95	_____
TEXAS TITLES				
_____	1-57071-330-8	How to File for Divorce in TX (2E)	$21.95	_____
_____	1-57248-114-5	How to Form a Corporation in TX (2E)	$24.95	_____
_____	1-57071-417-7	How to Make a TX Will (2E)	$16.95	_____
_____	1-57071-418-5	How to Probate an Estate in TX (2E)	$22.95	_____
_____	1-57071-365-0	How to Start a Business in TX (2E)	$16.95	_____
_____	1-57248-111-0	How to Win in Small Claims Court in TX (2E)	$16.95	_____
_____	1-57248-110-2	Landlords' Rights and Duties in TX (2E)	$21.95	_____

SUBTOTAL THIS PAGE _____

SUBTOTAL PREVIOUS PAGE _____

Shipping — $5.00 for 1st book, $1.00 each additional _____

Illinois residents add 6.75% sales tax _____

Connecticut residents add 6.00% sales tax _____

TOTAL _____

To order, call Sourcebooks at 1-800-432-7444 or FAX (630) 961-2168 (Bookstores, libraries, wholesalers—please call for discount)

Prices are subject to change without notice.